HISTORIC INNS
OF ENGLAND

TED BRUNING

Published in 2000 in Great Britain by
Prion Books Limited, Imperial Works, Perren Street,
London NW5 3ED

Text copyright © Ted Bruning 2000
Design and photography copyright © Prion Books 2000
Designed and edited by Bookwork
With photographs by Harry Lomax and Ted Bruning

A catalogue record for this book is available from the British
Library.

ISBN 1-85375-372-6

Printed in Singapore by Kyodo

A C K N O W L E D G E M E N T S :

This book would never have been written without the solid foundation
provided by the enthusiasm and work of local history societies, local
historians, and those breweries, hotel companies, and landlords keen
enough to delve into the antecedents of their pubs. I am extremely
grateful to all of them.

I would also like to thank the many friends who have helped in the
preparation of this book, especially my esteemed father-in-law Harry Levy,
Cressida Feiler, Roger Protz, Geoff Brandwood, and Roy Bailey; and
companies including Old English Inns, Forte Heritage Hotels, Arcadian
Hotels, the Savoy Group, Gale's Brewery, the Post Office Archives, Menzies
Hotels, Swallow Hotels, and The Great Inns Of England.

CONTENTS

HISTORIC INNS

The word "inn" is very evocative of English culture: of Chaucer, whose pilgrims set out from one; of Elizabeth I, who seems to have stayed in most of them; of Dickens, who saw them, literally and metaphorically, as havens on a hard and uncertain journey.

In England, talking of an inn conjures up images of rusticity, antiquity and nostalgia. The English will refer to a village or country inn, but they would never describe an otherwise identical urban establishment as anything but a pub. In America, the word has a different and historically more accurate meaning: there, a brand new motel can be described happily as an inn. This seems odd to English ears, but the best definition we have of the word, in an act of 1604, confirms the American usage. The purpose of an inn, it says, is the "receipt, relief, and lodging of wayfarers" – a service offered by few of the pubs the English might describe as inns. So, in the time of Chaucer, Elizabeth I and Dickens, the inn was the hotel of its day.

Above Sign of the Bull and Mouth.

For those who hold the traditional view of medieval society as largely static, this poses a problem. England's roads and towns are studded with inns that are undeniably medieval, and many more have been lost over the years – but who used them?

Actually, medieval society was far from static. Kings and their courts travelled constantly, consuming the produce of royal manors and forests, holding parliaments, doing justice, cowing the mighty and showing themselves to the people. Barons and prelates lived in the same way.

There was widespread trade in commodities. The country would have starved in winter without salt to preserve food, and most of it had to be carried from Cheshire and Worcestershire. Iron was another essential that had to be traded all over the country. The haulage of these goods involved large numbers of men who all had to be lodged and victualled, however primitively.

Warfare too brought plenty of travellers: parties of conscripts from the towns and levies from scattered baronial estates often had to travel long distances to the muster. These wayfarers required "receipt, relief and lodging" along the way.

Above The New Inn in Gloucester.

Increasing trade in finished woollens meant more traffic but also created a cash economy that generated still further trade in luxuries such as spices, lace, braid, jewellery and silks. Traders from merchant princes down to humble peddlers travelled the length and breadth of England, so the rutted roads of Merrie Englande were, if not seething, not deserted either.

Most if not all of the inns available to them were monastic foundations, built in pursuit of the charitable duty of hospitality. Every abbey, convent, friary and priory had its hospitium; larger ones had two, one for gentry and one for commoners. While these hospices were open to all, the travellers we most associate with them are those who, thanks to Chaucer, dominate our concept of medieval travel: pilgrims.

Pilgrimage had both spiritual and secular benefits. Prayers at the shrine of a martyr brought both grace and healing. Pilgrimage was for many the only chance of a break from a harsh routine, and to a serf, it even offered a chance of freedom. In theory, a lord could not prevent his serfs going on pilgrimage, and if they could stay away from the manor for a year and a day they were free.

There were dozens of places of pilgrimage across England: Westminster had the tomb of Edward the Confessor; Glastonbury the thorn tree of Joseph of Arimathaea; Gloucester the tomb of Edward II; Norwich, York, Lincoln, Hereford, Oxford and many other places also had relics attractive to pilgrims. But Canterbury was the greatest of them all. It was England's Compostela or Tours.

The Pilgrims' Way, which linked Canterbury with the west, was the most important route of pilgrimage. It started in Winchester, where pilgrims from the West Country, the Midlands and Wales, along with foreigners who disembarked at Southampton, joined up for a journey of more than 100 miles. Along the way were many places set aside by monks to receive travellers, some of them charitable hostels open free of charge, others rather better-appointed. In Winchester, poor pilgrims could lodge at the hospitals of St Cross or St John or at the Hundred Men's Hall. At Farnham there was Waverley Abbey, at Guildford the

Black Friars' hospice, and in Canterbury itself two abbeys, two friaries and two hospitals. All of these were free, decent and clean. But why sleep in a cheerless dormitory with a bellyful of refectory food when for 4d you could enjoy livelier company and something a deal more satisfying by way of victuals at the Godbegot at Winchester, the Bush at Farnham, the Angel at Guildford, and the Chequers, the White Hart (now the Falstaff) or the Sun in Canterbury?

At this point, the question of England's oldest inn raises its head. Many claim Saxon origin: the Godbegot was the hospice of St Swithun's Abbey in 1002; the Bingley Arms at Bardsey near Leeds was a "priests' inn" in 953; the Grosvenor at Shaftesbury was a monastic guest-house a century earlier. But the Godbegot has been through several major rebuildings; the Bingley Arms was pulled down and replaced in 1738; and the Grosvenor was rebuilt in 1836. So, although all have ancient foundations, what you see is comparatively recent. There is a clutch of 12th- and early 13th-century inns whose fabric is partly intact: the Oxenham Arms in South Zeal was a small canonry in about 1150; the Olde Bell at Hurley was also monastic and of similar date. There are many others of a similar vintage – and then there's the Trip to Jerusalem in Nottingham and its unsupported claim to a date of 1189.

The 13th and 14th centuries have left a good crop of monastic inns. The Green Dragon at Lincoln was the hospice of St Catherine's Priory in about 1300. The Crown at Chiddingfold, one of England's finest half-timbered inns and noted by Pevsner for its king-post roof, was an inn in 1383. The George at Norton St Philip was founded in 1397 by the monks of Hinton Charterhouse as both a guest-house and a warehouse and exchange for their estate's chief product, wool. Among its many distinctions, the George has a galleried courtyard, perhaps the first example of a plan that became more and more popular.

It has been said that the Crusaders brought the courtyard layout back with them in imitation of the arcaded pleasure-gardens of their enemies. The Saracens may have copied the idea from the Byzantines, who in turn inherited it from Rome – which would make Gloucester's New Inn a

distant cousin of the Roman villa at Fishbourne, Sussex. Alas, it's fantasy. The courtyard plan is common because it's the only practical way of utilising the typical long, narrow burgage plot; and the gallery is the best way of expanding in the only possible direction – upwards.

The George at Dorchester, the Star at Alfriston, the Angel & Royal at Grantham, the George & Pilgrims at Glastonbury – all these great 15th-century ecclesiastical inns seem to show that monasticism and pilgrimage were alive and well. They were not. Membership of monastic orders dwindled even as their wealth grew. The dissolution of the monasteries started as a moderate measure aimed at suppressing the more moribund orders and hardly seemed more than an act of rationalisation. But Henry VIII's government quickly developed an addiction to the injection of capital that came with each suppression: the first wave of closures of 1537 was followed by a second, more wide-reaching one. In March 1540, the last abbey in England, in Waltham, Essex, which had been founded by Harold Godwinsson five centuries before, closed its doors.

The dissolution put an end to the tradition of pilgrimage. It also released, through the sale of confiscated assets, hundreds of old-established monastic guest-houses, many of them already functioning as commercial inns, into what we might call the private sector. Despite the decline of pilgrimage, a new generation of merchants and other travellers created plenty of demand for accommodation, so the superior kind of hospice often carried on as before, but in private hands. For example Richard Bewforest, cousin of the last abbot of Dorchester-on-Thames, bought the abbey's estate for £150, gave the church itself to the parish, and settled back to enjoy the profits of its guest-house, now the George.

With businessmen like Bewforest in charge, the better-quality former guest-houses took on a new lease of life. It was a period of rising affluence and sophistication, and the inn trade did well. Many a fine house was turned into an inn: the Bull at Long Melford was a wool merchant's home until 1570; the Lion at Shrewsbury was a dwelling until 1618; the Feathers at Ludlow, built as a residence in 1603, was an

Left The Crown at Amersham.

inn by 1619. New inns were built, too: the George at Andover in 1546 and the George at Odiham in 1547.

The galleried design had made possible a great innovation: the private room. Had you arrived at the Crown at Chiddingfold or the Ostrich at Colnbrook in the 15th century, you would have eaten with the rest of the guests around trestle tables in the great hall. At night, with the trestles stacked away, you would have curled up to sleep in your cloak, perhaps on a straw mattress, quite likely on the rushes strewn on the floor. But sleeping on the rushes among fleas, rats, scraps of food, spilt ale and dog-droppings was only acceptable when nothing better was to be had. Once inns had begun to offer private chambers to the wealthy – although even they sometimes had to share – everybody wanted one. The new demand for privacy also led to the division of the eating and drinking accommodation into warrens of tiny parlours each with its own name: the Peacock, the Fleur-de-Lys, the Pomegranate, the Dolphin.

Competition was fierce and standards were high. One diarist, William Harrison, writing in 1583, was well-pleased with the inns he called at:

"Every man may use his inn as his own house. Each comer is sure to lie in clean sheets wherein no man has been lodged since they came from the laundress. If he lose aught while he abides at the inn, the host is bound by a general custom to restore the damage, so there is no greater security anywhere for travellers than in the greatest inns of England."

The testimony of two foreigners – a Dutchman and a Scot – is more flattering for being objective.

The Dutch doctor Levinus Lemnius, who visited England in the reign of Elizabeth, was almost embarrassingly effusive:

"The neat cleanliness, the exquisite fineness, the pleasant and delightful furniture in every point of the household wonderfully rejoiced me; the nosegays, finely intermingled with sundry sorts of fragrant flowers in the bedchambers and privy rooms, with wonderful smell cheered me up and entirely delighted all my senses."

The Scot, Fynes Moryson, writing in about 1620, described how on arriving at the inn, his travel-stained boots were whisked away to be cleaned while a fire was prepared in his room. For 6d or less he could eat a set meal at a communal table with the other guests, the landlord carving at its head. For a few pence extra he could have his food sent to his chamber. Musicians were employed to send the guests away in good humour in the morning, and he concluded that: "The world affords not such inns as England hath."

The best inns were often the finest buildings in the town, and many Justices of the Peace and other local authorities found them the most suitable places to do business: the George at Odiham, the George at Cranbrook, the White Bull at Ribchester, the New Inn at Pembridge, the Unicorn at Bowes, and the Speech House in the Forest of Dean all housed courts of one kind or another, as did many others, in some cases well into the 19th century.

Until this point, travellers who frequented the highways and inns of England did so under their own steam, as it were. There was no mass transit in the 17th century: you rode your own horse or drove your own new-fangled carriage. But in 1657 came an innovation that was to change all that: the first – or first recorded – public coach service. It ran between London and Chester three times a week, taking four days at a cost of 35s 6d. It was the beginning of the coaching era.

Coaching developed slowly and climaxed between 1784, when mail-coaches were introduced, and 1830, when the Post Office started using trains instead. It was the high point in the fortunes of England's inns. New ones were opened by the dozen, old ones were rebuilt by the hundred, and many of the attributes of the modern hotel, such as the large dining-room and the ballroom came into being. Thousands of inns made their living wholly or partly from coaching. At the height of the boom, more than 2,000,000 people travelled by stage-coach, mail-coach or post-chaise every year, and the inns had almost a monopoly on long-distance travel: even the rich who had their own vehicles depended on coaching inns for food, shelter and fresh horses.

Along with the development of coaching, the improvement of England's miry and rutted roads was essential to the prosperity of the inns. The process had a tentative beginning in 1555, when Mary I ordered parishes to levy a rate and conscript labour to maintain the highways. The state of the roads depended therefore on the wealth and energy available in the parishes through which they passed, which often left plenty to be desired. By the reign of James I, the roads were so poor that weight restrictions had to be imposed. As late as 1660, Ralph Thoresby had trouble following the Great North Road between Tuxford and Barnby Moor, and beyond Doncaster it petered out completely. This sorry state of affairs was not lost on hauliers, who often took a day to move a load four or five miles.

The first Turnpike Trust was set up in Hertfordshire in 1663, when a consortium of businessmen undertook to maintain a stretch of the Great North Road, funded by tolls. It was not an overnight success. Local opposition was fierce, and the second trust was not set up until the 1690s. At first, it was common for turnpikes to be set upon and destroyed: Hereford was gripped by riots when it was turnpiked in 1732. Nevertheless, between 1751 and 1772 nearly 400 new trusts were set up and, by the early 19th century, there were some 20,000 miles of turnpiked road.

Many of the trusts were run by businessmen and farmers concerned not to profit from the tolls but to secure their own interests – the transport of produce, as on the Corn Road from Hexham to Alnmouth, for instance, or the promotion of a resort. (Beau Nash was instrumental in the building of the London-Bath road in 1745.) In the main, such trustees could be relied on to discharge conscientiously, out of self-interest, a duty that benefited the whole community. But it was easy to tell where a turnpike was run by profiteers.

John Scott, in the *Digests Of The General Highway And Turnpike Laws* of 1778, bitterly attacked the system by which some trustees farmed out the upkeep of turnpikes to agents:

"The Trustees, once a road is farmed, have nothing to do but meet once a year to eat venison and pay the farmer his annuity: the farmer has nothing to do but work as little and pocket as much money as he

Above The White Bull at Ribchester.

possibly can; he has other matters to mind than road-mending. At length, perhaps, the universal complaint of travellers, or menaces of indictment, rouse the Trustees for a moment: a meeting is called, the farmer sent for and reprimanded, and a few loads of gravel buried among the mud serve to keep the way barely passable."

These are not charges that can be laid against the trusts that hired the three great road-builders of the age. Blind Jack Metcalfe of Knaresborough came to road-building from the haulage trade and built some 200 miles of turnpike in the 1750s to '60s, while Thomas Telford and John MacAdam, both Scottish, were almost exact contemporaries and did most of their work between 1810 and 1830. Between 1815 and 1817 Telford resurveyed the London-Shrewsbury-Holyhead road which, thanks to political lobbying, had some 30 years earlier displaced the Northern Road through Chester as the mail-coach route, but was still impassable in the more mountainous parts of North Wales. The Government contributed £20,000 towards the work, which thus became the first great public road-building scheme (other than the creation of Scotland's military roads after the Jacobite risings) since Roman times. MacAdam worked more in the South-West, where he was surveyor for the Bristol Turnpike Trust. His lasting achievement lay not in surveying new routes but in developing the cheap but reliable form of metalling which bears his name and is still in use today – tarmac.

By the end of the coaching era, more than 1,000 trusts were collecting £1.5 million a year from 8,000 tollgates. But from the 1840s income fell as coach services were superseded by the railways. From the 1860s, trusts were wound up as they came up for renewal. The last tollgate – on Telford's road in Anglesey – closed in 1895.

The coaches that ran on these roads were also constantly being improved. The ancestor of the coach was an unsprung palanquin brought from France by the Earl of Arundel in the reign of Elizabeth I. Such vehicles became fashionable after 1565, when the Queen herself was presented with one. Although she appeared on horseback before her troops at Tilbury during the Armada crisis, it was by coach that she made her many journeys about the country. Though these early carriages bounced, jarred and jostled, often got stuck in the deep mud and just as often broke down, so did riding-horses, and at least a coach saved the traveller from the worst of the weather.

By 1657, as we have seen, there was a regular public London-Chester service. Soon there were London-Kendal and London-Plymouth services as well, and a commentator in 1669 described them as possessing "an admirable commodiousness". Nevertheless, the trade made a hesitant start. Apart from the state of the roads themselves and the robbers who plagued them, the design of the coach was far from perfect. Arundel's was a clumsy, unsprung oaf of the road, little better than a covered wagon, and its successors were not much more than sedan chairs on wheels. A London service started by the landlord of the Pheasant in Shrewsbury in 1730 and dubbed the Gee-Ho was probably of the latter type, as was the coach shown in a Hogarth engraving of 1747. (A striking feature of this picture is that although there are no seats and no guard-rail, there are a few outsiders clinging on grimly and saved from falling off only by the coach's leisurely pace. Life for the outsiders was always tough, and the annals of coaching abound with tales of unfortunates found frozen to death at the end of a journey, or having their heads knocked off by low arches.)

By 1753, there were more services on the London-Shrewsbury road: the Long Coach was drawn by six horses and took four days, and Fowler's Stage took only three-and-a-half. The Diligence, started only 23 years later, did the journey in less than a day. Its secret was effective springing, which not only made it more comfortable but also increased its speed. Without it, coaching would never have reached its potential. The entrepreneur who first recognised and tackled the problem was Robert Lawrence, who took over the Raven in Shrewsbury in 1771, aged only 22, and became one of the most important figures in coaching.

Lawrence among the first to recognise the importance of punctuality, which had never been prized in a society largely without watches, but was essential to the efficiency of coach operators. If coaches

that were meant to arrive at 20-minute intervals arrived together, the result would be chaos. Lawrence's services were among those by which people swore they could tell the time – a cliché now, but a wonder then. He also started one of the first services to use efficiently sprung coaches and prove the value of the technology – the Shrewsbury-Birmingham Fly. In 1776 he launched the Diligence.

When Lawrence moved to the Lion in 1780, he took his business with him and, when in 1784, at the instigation of a theatrical impresario from Bath named John Palmer, the Government replaced the old system of mounted postboys with mail-coaches, Lawrence won the contract to service all mails passing through Shrewsbury. Long after his death in 1806, the Lion maintained the position in which he had left it. In 1825, it had seven daily coaches on the London-Holyhead run, 13 local services a day, and mail-coaches running to Chester, Welshpool, Newtown and Aberystwyth.

Lawrence was both pioneer and businessman, but he was not unique. By 1775, he and others like him had evolved the classic coach design that was to remain almost unchanged for more than 60 years, and were

Above The Lygon Arms in Broadway.

running some 400 main-road services with a fleet of nearly 17,000 vehicles. The introduction of mail-coaches in 1784 boosted the trade still further.

An official postal service was first created by Henry VIII, who contracted innkeepers to maintain the changes of horse for his dispatch riders. The innkeepers were paid 1d per mile per horse, reasonable under Henry VIII but not so good 100 years later. The innkeepers therefore took, illegally, to carrying private letters as well, a practice that was finally regularised in 1635 after an aggressive lobbying campaign headed by Thomas Hutchins of the George at Crewkerne in Somerset.

By Palmer's time the official postal service was less and less suited to the needs of business. Local postmasters reserved the most spavined old nags for the postboys, who were easy prey for the highwaymen who had plagued the roads since the Civil War. As a theatrical impresario, Palmer had already organised his own haulage business to enable his company to tour efficiently, and he believed a similar system could benefit the mail. On 2 August 1784, a trial run took place in a sprung vehicle with no outside passengers, and using fit horses changed every seven or eight miles. It cut the journey time between Bristol and London from 38 to 16 hours. The government was convinced. Within a year, mail-coaches from London were serving Norwich, Liverpool, Leeds, Dover, Portsmouth, Poole, Exeter, Gloucester, Worcester, Holyhead and Carlisle. In 1786, Palmer was made Surveyor and Comptroller General of the Post Office. In 1787 he approved the use of a patent coach built by a firm called Vidler's in Millbank, London. Its painted livery of black and maroon body and scarlet wheels soon became familiar throughout the land.

Although a Government service, the mail-coaches were mostly run by innkeepers who provided drivers and changes of team. Unlike commercial coaches, mail-coaches did not stop long enough at their stages for passengers to dine; they merely changed teams before ploughing on. They also travelled after dark and did not have to stop at tollgates – a blast on the guard's horn ensured the bar was raised in time

to let them through without slowing down. As a result they could average 7-8mph even before the road improvements of Thomas Telford and John MacAdam.

Unlike the driver, the guard, who wore a scarlet and blue coat with gold braid and black hat, was not an employee of the innkeeper-contractor, but of the Post Office. His horn was blown not just for tollgate keepers but also to warn ostlers, waiting with fresh teams, of his approach. At towns between stages, the mail-coach did not stop. The guard would throw out the bag of mail for delivery and snatch the bag for collection without the horses breaking stride. The guard also carried a short carbine with a distinctive bell-ended muzzle, known as a blunderbuss. Contrary to myth, the bell shape was not meant to scatter the shot more widely to increase the chance of a hit. It was purely to make reloading possible at high speed.

The highwaymen at whom the blunderbuss would be aimed were a menace for 150 years. The term predates the Civil War, but the upheavals it created made highway robbery endemic. A gin epidemic arrived in the 1690s with William III and cheap industrial-scale distilling. It lasted for a century and created generations of addicts who stole to fuel their habit. (Highwaymen were often arrested without a struggle, dead drunk, in exactly the drinking dens where the authorities expected to find them.) They were made more numerous by the Bloody Code, which, by prescribing the death sentence for minor crimes, meant petty thieves might, literally, just as well be hanged for a sheep as a lamb. It wasn't the Bloody Code that ended the scourge of highway robbery, either, (and it was a scourge: there was nothing romantic about Dick Turpin, who was a psychopath and torturer), but better policing and prudent measures such as the Limitation of Cash Payments Act 1797, which restricted the transportation of bullion: paper money was impossible for highwaymen to change. Jerry Abershaw, hanged at Kennington and gibbeted at Putney in 1795, was almost the last highwayman.

The golden age of coaching was also an age of rebuilding, during which the architectural face of the country was transformed. In most

Left The sign of the George & Dragon at West Wycombe.

market towns, if the principal inn was not Georgian, it would have been largely rebuilt or at least refronted in the 18th or early 19th centuries. The George in Rye, the Dolphin in Southampton, with its enormous bow-windows, the Sun in Hitchin, the White Hart in Lewes and the Lion in Shrewsbury, were among dozens of inns subjected to massive rebuilding between 1730 and 1780. In the last two decades of the century, an even grander style began to appear: the Angel in Bury St Edmunds, the Swan in Bedford and the White Hart in Salisbury all boast pillared porticoes the equal of many country houses.

These inns, with their ostlers and ever-ready fresh horses, their coffee-rooms, kitchens, private parlours and bedrooms, could afford to be choosy about their clientele, as Pastor Karl Moritz, a German who made a tour of Britain on foot in 1782, discovered. Travellers on foot were treated with suspicion, even hostility, and Moritz recorded that at one inn near Oxford, he was allowed to buy a drink but no food, and was curtly told to press on into the town itself, exhausted as he was, for lodging. Indignantly, he concluded:

"In England, a person undertaking a journey on foot is sure to be looked upon as either a beggar or a vagabond. It is impossible to approve of a system that confines all the pleasures and benefits of travel to the rich. A poor peripatetic is hardly allowed the humble merit of being honest."

His last comment is more revealing than he knew: snobbery was certainly a great motivator but, in a lawless age with no police force, so was fear.

The growing social segregation of the times meant that while gentry were prepared to use public inns, they did not expect to mix with the hoi polloi. The private rooms and coffee-room were reserved for those who travelled inside the coach; those who endured the hardships of the roof made do with the kitchen. Among the contemporary writers who remarked on this was Thomas de Quincey:

"It was the fixed assumption of the four inside people that they constituted a porcelain variety of the human race whose dignity would

have been compromised by exchanging one word of civility with the miserable delf-wares outside. What words then could express the horror and sense of treason in that case where all three outsides, the trinity of pariahs, made a vain attempt to sit down at the same breakfast table as the consecrated four?"

The principal inns soon became rallying points for polite local society, which did its best to emulate the high life of those centres of royal patronage, Bath and Brighton. The coaching inns were going up in the world, and soon acquired apartments to match their new-found status. Most of the larger inns boasted an assembly room, ballroom, or long room. Here, the hunt ball, the winter assemblies, the concerts, the

Above The Burford Bus outside the Old Bull in Burford.

exhibitions and all the other functions at which local gentry congregated took place. Frequently, these assembly rooms vied in proportion and ornament with the staterooms of the mansions of the rich: the Lion in Shrewsbury possesses a splendid assembly room, long held to be the work of the Adam brothers. In 1807, it entertained no less a personage than the Duke of Clarence, later William IV; in 1830 Madame Tussaud exhibited her waxworks there; in 1831 Paganini played there; and the Swedish Nightingale, Jenny Lind, sang there more than once. Jane Austen, David Garrick, Sir Joshua Reynolds and even George III were all entertained at the Bear at Devizes. The subscription dances at the Dolphin, Southampton, were well known: Jane Austen and her mother and sister spent the winter of 1808 there and were regular attenders, as were Clarence and the young Princess Victoria.

The end, when it came, was not as sudden as has been imagined. Rail took years to spread its tentacles over the country, and though the major coach routes were quickly killed off, local services lingered for 40 or 50 years. As late as 1844, a new coach service started running between London and Cambridge, and there were still hourly coaches between London and Brighton. Road mails were still calling at the Swan at Tewkesbury in 1864, and the Star at Lewes still ran coaches in 1874. The last commercial coach ran from the Crown at Amersham to London. It was little more than a bus really, and the opening of the Metropolitan line in 1894 finally killed it.

These survivals were, however, anachronisms. Trains were faster and cheaper than coaches and they took less than 15 years to kill the greater part of the trade. One of the better known closures was that of the Chapel House Inn on the Oxford-Birmingham road in 1850, where less than 70 years earlier Dr Johnson had told Boswell: "There is no private house in which people can enjoy themselves so well as in a capital tavern... There is nothing which has yet been contrived by man by which so much happiness is provided as by a good tavern or inn." When Charles Harper visited in 1903 the outbuildings had been made into cottages and the inn itself was a sort of B&B.

Innkeepers resorted to almost any shift to survive. In many cases, parts of the premises were sold or let: it is remarkable how many old coach offices, normally located beside the carriage arch, are now shops entirely separate from the inn. A wheelwright rented space at the George in Dorchester-on-Thames, and a tent-maker occupied the yard of the White Hart Royal in Moreton-in-Marsh. Stables became anything from warehouses to dairies, while the old coach-yards – the larger yard behind the narrow stableyard, where the coaches were oiled, washed and turned – were often sold as building plots, as were the gardens and orchards that many inns possessed. Yet it should not be forgotten that beyond the ticket-barrier, transport in Victorian England was horse-powered: there was still plenty of use for the stables of most inns. Many inns hired out gigs to travelling salesmen or ran livery stables; and inn yards proved ideal depots for local carriers whose businesses grew up to supplement the rail network, carting goods and passengers to outlying farms and villages right into the 1920s. But even when an old inn managed to limp along in this fashion, the glitter had worn off.

But it was not to be many decades before the honk of a motor-horn echoing down the lane heralded a new generation of road users and stirred many old inns back to life. Cars gave travelling salesmen a greater range than their gig-borne predecessors, creating a demand for commercial hotels for which many old coaching inns were ideal. Stableyards became garages and sprouted petrol pumps. Motoring organisations did an enormous amount to promote such inns and to raise standards, and even before the First World War a pleasure drive would almost certainly have taken in tea at some venerable inn. John Fothergill took this aspect of the business a stage further: having driven away the farmers who had previously haunted the Spreadeagle at Thame, he relied entirely on car-borne trade from Oxford and even London.

Fothergill, whom we shall meet not only at the Spreadeagle but also at the Three Swans in Market Harborough, was not one of a kind, as he has been portrayed, but one of a breed. Others were Sidney Bolton Russell, who revived the Lygon Arms in Broadway, Sir Clough Williams Ellis, architect of Portmeirion and restorer of the Mytton & Mermaid near Shrewsbury, and Walter Rye, who rescued the Maid's Head in Norwich. They were men of taste who recognised the potential of these splendid old inns and saw that there was a conservation-based strand in motor tourism that they could satisfy through raising standards. It was not only individual hoteliers who thought this way: in 1904, Earl Grey founded the Hertfordshire County Trust, the first of many such conservation bodies that eventually came together as Trust House Hotels, owning 150 of the most historic hotels and inns in the country before it was taken over by Forte in the 1960s.

Today, England's fine old inns are firmly embedded in the national aesthetic, attracting tourists and business people both British and foreign, serving fine food and drink in well-appointed and characterful surroundings and putting up guests in accommodation of international standards. (All but two of the inns featured in the book – the Ostrich, Colnbrook, Berkshire and the Waggon and Horses, Beckhampton, Wiltshire – continue to offer accommodation but you should always telephone to check first.) They range from great hotels like the George of Stamford to country pubs like the Cornish Arms at Pendoggett. But great or small, they all have that dictum of Moryson's to live up to: "The world affords not such inns as England hath."

Right The old coffee-room in the Talbot at Stourbridge.

BEDFORDSHIRE

SWAN
BEDFORD

The imposing Swan in its plum position at the crossing of the Ouse is one of the most handsome of the purpose-built coaching inns of the 18th century. But there was an inn on the site for at least 300 years before it was built.

Records of the earlier Swan go back to 1507 and, in the 17th century, it was used as chambers by judges on circuit. In 1674, a warrant was issued for "one John Bunnyon, tynker", for preaching against the Church of England, and it was to the Swan that his wife Elizabeth came to plead vainly with the judges for his release. While in Bedford Gaol, Bunyan wrote *The Pilgrim's Progress*.

The new Swan was commissioned in 1794 by the 5th Duke of Bedford, to take the coaching trade away from the rival Red Lion. He spared no expense, hiring one of the best architects of the day, Henry Holland. Two large bow windows overlook the Ouse, and the front is graced by a fine porch with a balcony and a great pediment resting on four ionic pillars. An elegant staircase with twisted balusters was installed inside, dating from 1688 and taken from the ruins of Houghton House, which, ironically, was Bunyan's model for the *House Beautiful*.

The Swan quickly became the town's principal inn, and has a connection with Bedfordshire's great brewing family, the Whitbreads: a grandson of Sam Whitbread ran the Bedford Times stage between the Swan and the Blue Boar, Holborn. Even after the railway came to Bedford in 1846, the Swan retained its position as the social centre for the local well-to-do. It was described by Sir Albert Richardson as "one of the most severe and correct of the later 18th-century inns ... the Swan has all the refinements of a sober Whiggish country mansion."

Above The Swan is a splendid classical building in lovely mellow stone.

BERKSHIRE

OSTRICH
COLNBROOK

The Ostrich is a contender for the title of England's oldest inn, claiming an origin of 1106, when it was given to Abingdon Abbey as a hospice (of which its name is a corruption) by one Milo Crispin, the gift being described as "*hospitium in via Londiniae apud Colebrok*".

The Ostrich was the setting for English literature's first crime novel, *The Clothier Of Reading*, written by Thomas Delaney in 1598. According to the story (and it is just a story), at some ill-defined point in the Middle Ages, the Ostrich's landlord, Jarman, devised a detection-proof method of robbing his wealthier patrons. He mounted a bed on a trap-door over a big vat of boiling water; plied the said wealthy patron with wine and showed him the best bed; and, once he was asleep, threw the lever operating the trap, and splosh! No more wealthy patron.

Eventually, of course, Jarman went a victim too far. He had been agonising over doing in a regular, Thomas Cole, the eponymous Clothier, for some time. Jarman's wife, a low-rent Lady Macbeth, nagged him into it; and into the stockpot went Thomas. The Jarmans were nicked while trying to dispose of Cole's horse, and ended up performing the Newgate rope-trick on a gallows made just for them outside the pub, which was then burnt down.

How the simple folk of Merrie England loved their bit of gore! – by 1632, *The Clothier Of Reading* had been through six editions.

What does ring true is that the Ostrich, owing to its proximity to Windsor, attracted a high class of guest even in the Middle Ages. King John stayed here on his way to Runnymede to sign – or seal – the Magna Carta, while ambassadors travelling from court would pause here for a

wash and brush-up and, if there was no room at the Castle, return here to sleep. Froissart says four ambassadors to Edward III "dyned in the King's chamber, and after they departed lay the same night at Colbrook".

With Colnbrook being 18 miles from Hyde Park Corner, the Ostrich became a stage on the Bath road, and both it and its many rivals flourished. "It is safe to assume," wrote Charles Harper in 1903, "that any important-looking old house facing the thoroughfare was once a hostelry." But, he added, the demise of coaching had made of Colnbrook "perhaps the best illustration of a coaching town ruined by railways that it is possible to discover."

Above What you see here is almost entirely Tudor.

Above The Georgian facade is more modern than the rest of the building.

BEAR
HUNGERFORD

Hungerford's Bear Hotel is a stereotype of coaching inns all over the country, with its Georgian classical facade, gabled porch, and bay windows concealing a much older foundation. It was first recorded in 1464 as being escheated to the Crown as part of the Manor of Chilton Foliat when the Duchess of Somerset died intestate. By this time, the Bear might already have been more than 250 years old, as it may have originally been the hospice of a monastery founded in 1232. The manor, and the Bear, remained in royal hands until the death of Henry VIII in 1547, when it was sold to a local landowner. The property had proved very useful to Henry: he bestowed it on five of his six wives.

The landowner who bought the manor from the Crown, Sir Edward Darrell, died two years later, and was succeeded by his son, Sir William. The notorious "Wild" Darrell, a ferocious man who made enemies of all his neighbours, led a lifestyle far beyond his means, conducted a love-affair with Lady Ann Hungerford of Hungerford Park, drank, fought, beat his wife, and finally dashed out the brains of a new-born baby he was accused of fathering. He was killed in a riding accident in 1589: the story is that his horse reared up at seeing the ghost of the murdered infant appear in the road before it, throwing Darrell and causing him the same injuries he had inflicted on the baby. The manor was inherited by one of his creditors, Sir John Popham, in whose family it remained until 1893.

At that time, the London-Bristol road passed north of Hungerford. Even so, the town was a convenient place to break a journey, and well-off and even royal travellers were prepared to make a detour to lodge at the Bear. They included Elizabeth I in 1601 and, in November 1644, Charles I, who made the Bear his headquarters for the relief of Basing House. Charles II tarried here twice, in 1663 and 1665; his queen, Catherine of Braganza, and James II's queen, Mary of Modena, also stayed. In 1688, the royal guest was William of Orange, who held talks with James II's commissioners here. The talks were a disaster for James: he fled into exile forever immediately after.

The main road was finally rerouted through Hungerford in 1744; the Bear immediately became a very busy stage on the London-Bath road, catering for 50 coaches a day from a yard covering two acres. Pitt the Elder, Beau Brummell, Nelson, and both George III and IV were among the patrons who alighted here while horses were changed. Sidney Smith once ordered seven dinners here for a friend of his, a pluralist who was a dean, an archdeacon, a canon, a prebendary, a vicar, a rector, and a curate.

All this activity died almost overnight when the railway came in 1847; but the Bear survived on the custom of private carriages and the residual business snapped up from failed competitors. And, of course, the railway generated some custom: in 1891, the tenant, William Rennie, was hiring out flies to commercials brought to Hungerford by train.

Rennie bought the Bear from the Pophams in 1893 for £1,500, but soon fell ill and sold it to a local brewery. Despite brewery ownership, it remained a very superior place – Evelyn Waugh, Dennis Wheatley, and Alfred Munnings were among its clients. It was bought from the brewery in 1953 and changed hands a number of times thereafter. It is now part of Jarvis Hotels.

YE OLDE BELL

HURLEY

How old does an inn have to be before it becomes Olde; and is Olde not an abomination which should never be permitted, however Olde the inn in question might be? Well, Ye Olde Bell claims a date of origin of 1135; so if any inn is entitled to call itself Olde, the Bell is. I do not know what evidence supports the date, but the Bell claims to have been the guest-house of the Priory of Lady Place 250 yards away, founded in 1086 by Geoffrey de Mandeville.

Above The large, imposing sign is typical of many coaching inns.

The Bell is one of those places supposedly linked to its parent house by underground passage. If you believed all such tales, you'd be afraid to walk about for fear of subsidence. I do not believe that medieval monks really indulged in subterranean perambulations that can have brought no practical benefit. Until proved wrong, the most I will allow is that the so-called tunnel entrance one is often shown in inn cellars is no more than additional cellarage.

The Bell may be old enough to be Olde but, other than a Norman doorway, what you see is almost entirely early 16th-century. It is filled with oak panelling and ancient beams, and its wonderful ornamental gardens have long been rightly famous. It has also pleased generations of connoisseurs: Charles Harper in the 1920s called it "a very delightful old inn," adding: "You will get more than bread and cheese for lunch at the Bell, to say the least of it; the house is 500 years old, but not the management." Denzil Batchelor, 40 years later, praised the Austrian chef, the Continental waiters in plum-coloured livery, and the standard of food, although he added: "You pay for eating in the 12th century, but no-one on expenses or from Texas should miss it." Nearly 40 years on again, the Bell has the rare accolade of an AA rosette to go with its three stars.

Above The Bell.

Above The yard reveals the Crown's true antiquity, with its timber frame and low roof.

BUCKINGHAMSHIRE

CROWN
AMERSHAM

I f you had to rank Old Amersham's inns by picturesque appearance, you would probably put the gabled, half-timbered King's Arms above the rather severe neo-classical Crown. But just as you shouldn't judge a book by its cover, so you shouldn't judge a coaching inn by its frontage. For beneath its skin of Georgian brick lies a fine 16th-century inn.

Inside, the Crown's Tudor origins are obvious, with beams and panels in plenty. There is even a coat of arms of Elizabeth I in the lounge – sadly only a reproduction, since the original was damaged by fire in 1935. The reason given for the coat of arms being there is that it commemorates a visit by the monarch to a nearby nobleman's house. However, it is also recorded that the Crown hosted the town's petty sessions from Elizabeth's reign until 1879 and, as those unlucky enough to have appeared before the beak will know, magistrates and judges always sit beneath the royal coat of arms. Maybe the court was held not in the room now called the Court Bar, but here in the lounge?

Another, and truly remarkable, survival of Elizabethan times is the wall-painting in room 12, where an abstract pattern is repeated over and over again to cover one wall.

From prosperous town inn, the Crown graduated to even more prosperous coaching inn in the 18th century, when the brick front was added. Amersham was two stages from London on the southern route to Aylesbury, Birmingham, and, ultimately, Liverpool. Its broad high street was thronged with coaches and lined with inns. The Crown is almost the last survivor: here, the coaching era can be said to have come to its end in 1894, when the last regular horse-drawn coach service – to and from the Old Bell, Holborn – was finally put out of business by the Metropolitan Line.

COCK
STONY STRATFORD

The Cock being, as it is, a 31-bedroom, three-star Georgian coaching inn of distinction, boldly looking out on a Roman road and with a proud record of service down the centuries, it must be a little galling for its owners to know that its name is synonymous with claptrap.

But that's how it is, for the Cock is one half of the "cock and bull story" of cliché, the other half of the name being supplied by the Bull, another leading coaching inn in the town.

There are, as always in cases like this, many derivations of the expression. Even Harper let his halo slip here. "It is an article of faith at Stony Stratford that the term derived from the often misleading items of news exchanged from talk heard from the up and down coaches at the Cock and Bull inns at either end of the town," he wrote in the 1920s. The Bull, however, is next door but one, not at the other end of town.

A more recent writer, John Burke, says that the expression arose as a description of loose talk during the Napoleonic War, but goes no further. The inn's own leaflet says that coach travellers staying at the two inns used to vie with other in yarn-spinning, begging the question: where? Did they have home and away fibbing fixtures? Did they meet on the pavement outside? Sorry, no cigar. But as there is no evidence to explain the term, then all theories are cock and bull. Which is half the fun.

The Cock is first recorded in the 15th century, when its rent funded local good works. In the 17th century, when lacemaking was a major

Above The Cock's high coach arch looks on to Roman Watling Street.

industry in the area, the Cock's landlord acted as a middleman between the weavers and the dealers who bought their work. The old Cock was destroyed in 1742 by a fire started, they say at the Cock, by a maid at the Bull who burnt a sheet while ironing and tried to hide it up a chimney. The inn was rebuilt in the soft red brick that is one of the glories of the English Midlands. A magnificent 17th-century carved oak doorcase, in the style of Grinling Gibbons, was imported from a nearby mansion, Battlesden Park, as an imposing front door. The wrought-iron sign bracket, another of the wonders of the inn, is also thought to date from the mid-18th century.

At the height of the coaching era, 100 coaches a day passed through Stony Stratford. The Manchester Flier, which left London at 8.30am and arrived in Manchester at 5.10am next day, only allowed 25 minutes for lunch at the Cock, so passengers had to eat fast. Among them, on more than one occasion, was Charles Dickens, who based Mr Turveydrop in *Bleak House* on a local dancing instructor, Joseph Hambling.

Steam left Stony Stratford high and dry, but cars produced a revival. My father, a commercial traveller who often passed through Stony Stratford in the 1930s, claimed that the name "Watling Street" was nothing to do with Romans or Saxons, but was coined by the commercial fraternity. They would greet each other at watering-holes like the Cock with a cry of: "What'll ye have, old boy? What'll ye have?" Yes, yes; it's another cock and bull story ...

Above The interior archways mirror the impressive coach arch outside.

GEORGE & DRAGON
WEST WYCOMBE

A sad place, West Wycombe. Strung out along a narrow cleft between sudden outcrops of Chiltern limestone, its dusty glories go unnoticed by the thousands of motorists who thunder through each day. Yet almost every building lining the narrow A40 is a treasure, the early Georgian red-brick George & Dragon being the finest.

West Wycombe is best-known as the headquarters of that ludicrous group of 18th-century wannabe degenerates, the Hell Fire Club. Really, the Hell Fire Club was no more than a coterie of drunks and gamblers

Above The low coach arch dates the inn to the early part of the 18th century.

who would also, on the rare occasions when desire and ability coincided, indulge in a spot of whoring. What made them fearsome to the local peasantry was that they held their boozy beanos in a sinister network of caves, which had once been lime-quarries, dressed up as demons, warlocks, monks, and so forth.

Probably, the Hell Fire Club never really meant anyone any harm; but people are so easily hurt. Sukie, a comely maid at the George & Dragon, fell for the smooth words and fat purse of one of the blueblood Bacchanalians. He took advantage; she mistook his attentions for love and spurned her own swain, who, to teach her a lesson, lured her to a spurious rendezvous with her well-heeled lover in the caves, where a salutary beating was handed out. It all got out of hand, and Sukie haunts the George & Dragon to this day.

You don't need a ghost story to lure you to the George & Dragon. Built in 1720, it's a lovely example of an early coaching inn, its low arch betraying its date – archways were commonly raised in the latter part of the century to accommodate the outsiders carried by later coaches.

Harper described West Wycombe as "the very model of what an old coaching thoroughfare village was like", adding: "The old semi-urban character of the great road to Oxford has, with the passing of the coaches, long become merely a memory. West Wycombe once called itself a town, but cannot nowadays make that claim convincingly. If we call it a decayed coaching town, that is the most that can be conceded, for today its every circumstance is rustic.

"The George & Dragon, a glance at its imposing front is sufficient to show, was built for the great, or those great enough to be able to command the price of chaise-and-four and sybarite accommodation; but the passing stranger would nowadays be unlikely to secure any better meal than bread and cheese, and the greater part of the house is silence and emptiness, while the once bustling yard has subsided into picturesque decrepitude."

One wonders whether the revival of road traffic through the town, in the form it has taken, would have pleased him.

CAMBRIDGESHIRE

HARDWICKE ARMS
ARRINGTON

Elegant, timeless, serene, the Hardwicke Arms stands on ancient ground beside the old coach road. Ermine Street, on which the Hardwicke stands, is a pre-Roman trackway, straightened and surfaced by the legions, and an inn has stood here since the 13th century. Called the Tiger in the 17th and 18th centuries, it was extensively made over in 1760, when it was almost totally rebuilt by the architect of Wimpole Hall, Sir John Soane. His innovations included an ingenious central heating system using hot air ducts radiating from the massive chimney in the middle of what is now the private dining-room.

Its situation and amenities guaranteed the Hardwicke Arms – as it was renamed – an excellent trade, not just as a coaching and posting-house, but also as an overflow for Wimpole Hall's guests and their horses and servants. In 1793, it was rented by William Usdell, former butler at the Hall, and in 1806, it became a Post Office, which ensured the custom of the mail coaches on Ermine Street.

The collapse of coaching left this isolated inn stranded. There was still custom from the Hall, but little else; even the motor-car did little to revive the inn's fortunes.

In the 1920s, Charles Harper wrote: "Close at hand are the great avenues of Wimpole, the lordly park created by the first Earl of Wimpole in the early 18th century: the Hardwicke Arms which now stands forlorn by the roadside owes its existence to the comings and goings, the bustle and stir, caused by my lord's vast hospitalities. Long ago they

Left The ivy-clad Georgian front exudes permanence and solidity.

ceased, and Wimpole is silent. It is a lonely road, and the Hardwicke Arms would seem to have been set down here from mere fantasy, did we not know the story."

At this time, the old coach-house and stables behind were used as farm buildings, and the inn had its own farm and orchard. After the Wimpole estate sold it in 1932, the Hardwicke Arms survived as a brewery-owned beerhouse, and bits and pieces were gradually sold to keep it afloat. The coach-house is used today as the village hall; the orchard is a nursing home; six houses stand on the old coach yard; and there are houses on its old paddock.

In the 1980s, the inn changed hands several times; finally the recession of the early 1990s proved too much and, in October 1991, it closed. It stood empty until May 1993, when it was bought, restored, and eventually reopened as a comfortable inn, with a splendidly atmospheric dining-room, an olde-worlde bar, and correct attention paid to the important matter of beer.

Above The creeper-clad Georgian White Horse inn stands on 15th-century foundations.

WHITE HORSE
EATON SOCON

St Neots in the 18th century was a focal point for the coach trade: it stood at a crossing of the Ouse where routes from Cambridge and Bedford joined the Great North Road. As the market town for a prosperous agricultural region, it also generated traffic in its own right.

Of the three coaching inns once in the town centre, the Bridge Inn is a steakhouse; the rambling Falcon is a beerhouse; and the ancient Cross Keys is a shopping mall. On the Great North Road itself, the Brampton Hut has vanished under an interchange of the A1. Only the White Horse survives, fronting a suburban street rather than the national aorta this stretch of road once was.

Refounded as a posting house in the early 18th century, the White Horse did not become one of the great coaching inns until an extension was added two or three generations later. Sir Albert Richardson identifies

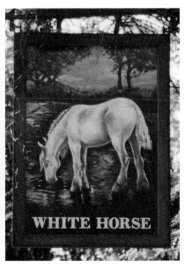

the picturesque original as the model for the Black Lion in Smollett's *Sir Launcelot Greaves* and the inn in Goldsmith's *The Deserted Village*. Smollett describes its kitchen, thus: "paved with red bricks, remarkably clean, furnished with three or four Windsor chairs, adorned with shining plates of pewter and copper saucepans nicely scoured; a cheerful fire of sea-coal blazed in the chimney."

In 1838, the inn played host to Dickens, He was so struck with the White Horse that he used it, under the guise of the Cock, Eton Slocomb, for the scene in which Squeers and his caravan of doomed boys break their northward journey to dine.

Above The modern sign hangs from an 18th-century wrought iron bracket.

BELL
STILTON

However well-sited, well-appointed, and well-known they may be today, many of England's leading inns only just survived the coming of steam in the 1840s. To visit the renowned Bell at Stilton today, you would never guess how far it fell.

The Bell, of course, is famous as the birthplace of Stilton cheese – which actually came from Melton Mowbray but was adopted as the house speciality by the early 18th-century landlord, Cooper Thornhill.

Not everyone liked the cheese: Defoe said it was "called our English parmesan, and brought to the table with the mites round it so thick that they bring a long spoon for you to eat the mites with, as you do the cheese." But enough people liked it to order extra portions to take away with them; eventually a wholesale business was set up, and the fame of Stilton cheese was assured.

The Bell was not the town's principal inn: Stilton was a main stage on the Great North Road with several prominent inns. The Angel was much larger, with stabling for 300 horses; the Talbot and the Woolpack were also bigger; as was the Norman Cross just north of the town. However, the Bell was a prosperous business at the end of the coaching era.

The end of coaching hit it hard: it was, according to one writer in the late 19th century, "gaunt, ghost-like, deserted, half alive", and Charles Harper, in 1903, found that this "fine old house with a still finer old sign, formerly one of the largest and most important of the many great inns that once ministered to the needs of travellers along the Great North Road" was now a mere alehouse where "they look at you with astonishment when you ask to stay the night, and turn you away."

Motoring brought a revival in the Bell's fortunes, as trade began once more to flow past its doors; then Stilton was by-passed, and it was back to the old case of out of sight, out of mind. The pub actually closed down in the 1970s. Fortunately, it has since been restored and reopened in the style it deserves.

Right The Bell sports a huge and intricate sign bracket.

HAYCOCK
WANSFORD

ansford was, for centuries, the place where the Great North Road crossed the Nene: the earliest mention of its bridge is in 1221, when indulgences were granted to anyone who helped pay for its upkeep. It may be that the Haycock started its chequered career at this time, for a lintel in the old Smoke Room is

Above The Haycock's slate roof extends for more than an acre.

thought to date back to the reign of John. But the first record of the pub is not until 1571, when there was an inn called the Swan on the site.

The present building, according to a date-stone found in the garden, was erected in 1632. It was clearly a house of importance even then, with stabling for 150 horses – probably pack-ponies rather than coach-horses – and an impressive Collyweston slate roof.

The last mention of the Swan is in 1706; by 1712, the inn was the Haycock and the village was Wansford-in-England. The story behind the changes relates to the legendary toper Drunken Barnaby, who was sleeping off a binge on a haystack when the Nene was flooded by the Collyweston slaters to float their barges. Barnaby woke to find that he and his stack were being washed "down the current; people cried, As along the stream I hied, 'Where away,' quoth they, 'from Greenland?' 'No, from Wansford Bridge, in England!'" Viscount Torrington, journeying round the country a century later, noted that the original Barnaby sign from 1712 was still there.

The innkeeper in 1808, Jeremiah Mallatratt, lost the property at cards to one Anthony Percival, who hugely extended the inn and died in 1826. In 1841, his widow handed the inn over to their son Thomas, who had been an important figure in coaching days and who founded White's Club in 1859. After his death in 1878, his widow Elizabeth ran the inn as a beerhouse, the railways having killed the coaching trade in the '50s; but her main business was farming the Haycock's 625 acres. In 1893 – having, according to Charles Harper in 1903, "bravely kept its doors open until recent years" – the pub finally closed.

In 1898, it was bought by Lord Chesham as a hunting-box. Among its many guests were the Duke and Duchess of Teck, George V's parents-in-law; but during World War I, the stables, coach-house, brewhouse, and other outbuildings bade farewell to hunters and grooms and became an ammunition factory.

With the growth of motoring in the mid-1900s, the inn was reopened as a first-class hotel in 1928, and was a favourite haunt of USAAF airmen during the Second World War.

Above The late 17th-century timber framing is unusually elaborate and sophisticated.

CHESHIRE

BEAR'S HEAD
BRERETON

The Bear's Head is a fine example of the splendid half-timbered buildings for which Cheshire is famous. Timber-framing was common in Cheshire in the late 1800s, when other areas had run out of oak.

The Bear's Head dates from 1615, according to an inscription on the tall porch, with its arched doorway and large gable, on which are also carved the initials WB, for William Brereton, and the Brereton arms. Originally, this was the Brereton's manor, becoming an inn when the family built itself a grander house: Brereton Hall, the model for Washington Irving's *Bracebridge Hall*.

The A50, on which the inn stands, was then the London-Liverpool road, and the Bear's Head soon became a prominent coaching and posting inn. A pleasant if undistinguished extension was added at the height of the inn's prosperity; but you will look in vain for the coachyard, for the Bear's Head has none. A magnificent brick stable-block was built across the road, with a central pediment supported by two pilasters over the main arch and projecting wings at the rear. Although a yard behind the inn was the usual arrangement, it was by no means universal, especially where an entirely new stable-block had to be added to an existing site. Alas, the Bear's Head's stables have long been pulled down – don't be fooled by the bedroom wing, which is built of old brick and looks for all the world like converted stables: it was built about 30 years ago to look like that.

LION & SWAN
CONGLETON

Congleton is one of those picturesque industrial towns that predate steam. Unlike the great cities of the 19th century – Leeds, Sheffield, Manchester – the earliest manufacturing towns were small and situated in valleys where there was plenty of water pressure to turn the millwheels. Unlike Leeds or Manchester, they often preserved remnants of the country market towns they had once been.

Congleton was just such an old market town when the millwright James Brindley, more famous as the country's first great canal-builder in the 1760s and '70s, dug a loop from the River Dane to power a silk mill, transforming it into a cradle of industry. Was it then or earlier that the 16th-century half-timbered home of the Alsager family was converted into an inn? Whenever it was, the Lion & Swan – the name derives from the union of two licences rather than a coat of arms – soon started attracting its share of the posting trade brought by Congleton's burgeoning fortunes.

The Lion & Swan was never quite as busy a coaching inn as the Bull's Head; but after 1840, the whole question became academic. Not only did the railways ruin the coach trade, but the original main road was moved so the Lion & Swan was no longer even on it.

But an industrial town such as Congleton had plenty of use for a distinguished and comfortable inn; the Lion & Swan soldiered on, lodging not only commercial visitors but also tourists, for though the town itself had become industrial, it was still set in some of England's most glorious upland countryside.

Among the tourists in the early years of the 20th century, was Charles Harper, who was normally very sniffy about anything urban, but described the half-timbered Lion & Swan as "a wonder of that magpie kind of construction." It was, he wrote, "one of the best and most picturesque features of that old-time manufacturing town, more remarkable for its huge old factory buildings and its narrow sett-paved

streets in which the clogs of the workfolk continually clatter, than for
its beauty. The Lion & Swan, therefore, is a distinct asset in the
picturesque way, with its beautiful black-and-white gables and strongly
emphasised entrance porch. Within it is all timbered passages and
raftered rooms, pleasantly irregular."

A striking interior feature, which Harper was too delicate to mention,
is the magnificent intricately-carved oak Tudor fireplace in the old
cocktail bar, graphically depicting fertility and childbirth.

Above The Lion & Swan escaped the addition of a Georgian facade.

OLD HALL

SANDBACH

From the road, the Old Hall looks too grand to be a mere inn: its black-and-white gables of oak from the Mondron Forest gaze out serenely on the marketplace and its Saxon crosses, like the great house of some ancient blue-blooded family – which, as the name suggests, is just what it was.

Above The interior of the Old Hall still has a homely atmosphere.

The house that stood here in medieval times was a fortified manor: survivors from those days are a barn in the yard at the back and a spiral staircase with a right-hand twist, to free the sword arm of the retreating defender, while hampering that of an attacker advancing from below.

It was replaced by the present building in 1656, when it belonged to the Earls of Crewe. Much of the panelling, the exposed oak beams, and the three fireplaces, with their carved overmantels appear to date from this period.

In time, the Earls abandoned it for grander quarters – though they retained the freehold until recently – and, as often happened, it became an inn. Being well-sited and well-equipped, it soon attracted a brisk coaching and posting trade. It survived the end of coaching as a humble beerhouse, brewing for regulars and for local farmers, who still paid partly in kind, until World War I made the materials too scarce. Charles Harper, in 1903, sampled the ale, judging it "a very pretty tipple". It also had a pair of dog-gates across the top of the staircase, which kept the hounds – not housetrained in the 17th century! – out of the family quarters. These had to be removed to satisfy fire regulations when the Old Hall reopened its letting rooms.

Above The timbered front survives from the mid 1600s.

Above The plain Georgian front hides a far older building.

CORNWALL

PUNCHBOWL
LANREATH

Although it has only held a licence since 1620, the Punchbowl is a place of huge antiquity: parts of it are thought to be 13th century and the well, on which it relied for water, is much older. This is one of those wells which was locally credited miraculous healing properties; its name, St Monarch's Well, possibly comes from the Latin *monachus*, meaning monk.

In these parts, the veneration of springs and wells goes back much further than Christianity and St Monarch's Well may have been a sacred site long before the Christians claimed it. Sadly, this well has been covered over; to add insult to injury, the gents has been built on top of it, so the libations you pour there are not likely to please St Monarch.

The oldest part of the present building is at the rear and was originally a longhouse of two rooms, one for the family and one for the livestock, divided by a central passageway. It may date from the 13th century; but the pattern, common throughout Devon and Cornwall, is almost timeless so, whatever its actual date, it connects with an era long predating our own. The front rooms were added in the 16th or early 17th century, at about the time when the Punchbowl graduated from farmstead to inn and began a new period of prosperity.

For many years, it served as the local courthouse, as did many inns. Two waiting rooms were set aside, one for commonfolk and one for gentry, where they could refresh themselves while awaiting their day in court. The two rooms are now bars, known as the Farmers' Kitchen and the Men's Kitchen. In coaching days, the village stood on the Looe-Fowey road, and the Punchbowl enjoyed some posting trade. What is now a passageway was once the carriage arch, leading to the stableyard, and the frame of one window is made of a carriage wheel.

CORNISH ARMS
PENDOGGETT

There is nothing especially historical about the Cornish Arms. It's just a small posting-house, maybe 17th century, but maybe much older, on a quiet offshoot of the main coach road from Bath to Truro. But, compared to the rich fare provided by the majority of England's architecturally glorious coaching inns, with their heavy seasoning of historical and literary associations, it's the perfect palate-cleanser.

It has bedrooms, seven of them, so it qualifies as an inn. It's known for its food, too: it was commended nearly 40 years ago by the cricket writer Denzil Batchelor for the quality of its cooking. It is still well-known for its fine dining-room specialising in freshly-landed fish from Port Isaac a couple of miles away. But essentially, the Cornish Arms is a pub – and what a pub.

Inside, floors of Delabole slate, heavy oak beams, and crackling log fires make the perfect setting for beers drawn straight from the cask. Outside, its low stature, coat of render and cape of hanging slates testify to the battering that winter can hand out here, just a mile from the Atlantic as the gull flies.

Indeed, those who think of Cornwall as a summer destination might look at the Cornish Arms and think again: those fires aren't just for ornament or atmosphere.

As Thomas Burke once wrote: "In winter the inn allures us. It is not merely shelter and refreshment: it is a beatific image of contrast.

Outside are snow, ice, fog, or rain, wind, and mire. Inside, your imagination says, are glowing hearths, piquant odours, lights, drawn curtains, and soothing chairs. Indeed, most of our inns appear to have been designed with an eye only to hard weather, their narrow passages, low ceilings, small rooms, huge fireplaces and shuttered windows all making for snugness."

He could have been talking about the Cornish Arms.

Above The little inn seems to huddle down against the weather.

CUMBRIA

BLACK BULL
CONISTON

What could be more perfect than a four-poster bed in a room in a 400-year-old coaching inn set in some of England's most spectacular scenery, and possessing a brewery that produces Britain's best beer?

Stop dreaming … it's real! The inn in question is the Black Bull at Coniston in the Lake District – the beck that feeds Lake Coniston runs beside the hotel, and rising behind it is the fell known as the Old Man, whose Big Toe is actually a breakaway boulder embedded in the wall of the residents' lounge.

The Black Bull's earliest customers were the miners who dug for copper in the fells. The Lake Poets were no strangers to the inn, although Wordsworth actually lived some way away at Grasmere. The artist Turner also visited to the Black Bull, and another artist, John Ruskin, became slowly more and more demented in his long retirement at Brandwood House in Coniston itself. A more recent guest, just as tragic in his way, was the daredevil Donald Campbell, who lost his life attempting the world water speed record on Lake Coniston in 1967. Some of the scenes in the film of his last record attempt, *Across The Lake*, were filmed at the Black Bull.

So much for guests: the inn's present ruling dynasts, Ron Bradley and his son Ian, have an achievement of their own, which will also go down in history.

Ron bought the inn off a local brewery in 1975 and, having run it peaceably for 20 years, was tempted to try some home-brewed beer at a pub in Sussex. He was so impressed that nothing would satisfy him but to start a brewery of his own. An annexe was earmarked as a brewery; bits and pieces of kit were hunted down hither and yon;

and young Ian, never having brewed a drop in his life, was packed off to college to learn how.

In October 1995, Ian's 13th trial brew was deemed fit for public consumption. A pale gold bitter of 3.6 per cent alcohol, with a massive orangey dose of Challenger hops, Blue Bird was soon selling 20 brewer's barrels a week – that's 720 gallons to laymen – at the Black Bull and in 15 neighbouring pubs. If that wasn't enough, in August 1998, the Campaign for Real Ale named Blue Bird its Champion Beer of Britain. And yes, you can book a room there. You can go fell-walking there. You can enjoy an evening stroll by Coniston Water there. And you can drink the best beer in Britain there. It's not just a dream.

Above The inn nestles at the foot of the Old Man fell.

Above In the 1700s, the inn's front was rebuilt in the fashionable classical style.

GEORGE
KESWICK

Keswick has been England's most popular inland resort since the Romantic poets adopted the Lake District 200 years ago. But before that, it depended partly on the manufacture of pencils, which began in 1566, and partly on the silver mines developed by Bavarian migrants, who first arrived in 1561. By this time, the George & Dragon, as it was, was already Keswick's principal inn and one of its most imposing buildings. It was, therefore, the natural choice for the counting-house and revenue office for the silver brought down by packmule from the Goldscope and Borrowdale deposits, which the Germans were working. For 80 years, until the seams were exhausted, Keswick must have resembled a western boom-town, an impression heightened by a lively black market in ore, filched by the miners before duty could be levied on it.

The inn dropped the dragon from its title on the death of Queen Anne, becoming the plain George in honour of the new dynasty. The following year, the Earl of Derwentwater, who lived on Lord's Island in the lake on which Keswick stands, went to join the rebels; the last the town saw of him was when he popped into the inn for a farewell beer. A year later, he was beheaded on Tower Hill.

Later that century, the smugglers were back at the George: in 1752, the export of graphite, then known as wadd or plimbago and used in the manufacture of gunmetal, was banned. A brisk trade promptly sprang up, with the George as a main centre of exchange between those who mined the "pipes" and the foreign buyers who carried the booty down to the sea at Ravenglass in exchange for contraband liquor.

Later in the century, the George became a prominent coaching inn. In 1800, Coleridge arrived, to be followed by Southey. Keats, de Quincey, and Charles Lamb were all frequent visitors; and Shelley lived in a cottage on Chestnut Hill. It would be surprising if they did not know the George well, as it was the area's main coaching station.

DERBYSHIRE

GREEN MAN & BLACK'S HEAD ROYAL
ASHBOURNE

The Green Man, as it is generally known, was first recorded only in 1710, when a new organ was dedicated at the parish church. Choirs from Lichfield and Lincoln Cathedrals accompanied by brass and strings, as well the new organ, performed at the ceremony and were afterwards feasted at the Green Man where, after a generous fluid intake, they gave an impromptu concert.

Above The gallows sign was erected after a visit by Princess Victoria.

By that time the hotel had established a leading role in local affairs, hosting the Magistrates' Court for the Low Peak Hundred. It also had a cockpit, even though cockfights were always attended by furious and completely illegal betting, of which the Justices must surely have been aware (if indeed they didn't have a punt themselves).

In 1777, Dr Johnson and Boswell stopped for lunch here: Boswell reported that it was a good inn with a "mighty civil landlady" who presented him with an engraving of the inn-sign and also wrote him a rather fawning note not untypical of the times: "Mrs Killingley's duty awaits upon Mr Boswell; is exceedingly obliged to him for this favour; whenever he comes this way hopes for a continuance of the same. Would Mr Boswell name this house to his extensive acquaintance, it would be

a singular favour conferred upon one who has it not in her power to make any other return but her most grateful thanks and sincerest prayers for his happiness in time and in blessed eternity."

The cumbersome name results, as so often with double-barrelled pubs, from the union of two licences. The Green Man took over the licence of the Blackamoor's Head some way up the street, last recorded as a separate inn in 1802. The landlord of the Green Man at the time, Mr Brooks, also added the last name to the inn's title after a visit by Princess Victoria and her mother.

At about that time, an ancient tradition was revived. Shrove Tuesday Football is a furious scrum involving the Up'ards from north of Hensmore Brook and the Down'ards from south of it, in an attempt to score between stone goal-posts set three miles apart.

Huge muslin-wrapped joints of meat, for the inn's kitchen and for butchers in the town, were once hung from hooks on the carriage arch. The muslin protected the meat from flies, while the current of air through the arch dried, preserved, matured and tenderised it.

RUTLAND ARMS
BAKEWELL

The story of coaching is littered with stories of ancient inns modernised – mullioned casements replaced with sashes, gothic stone fronts plastered over or given a skin of smart red brick, and new wings added in the classical style. But it is comparatively rare to find an antique inn completely torn down and replaced, as happened here.

The White Horse was a well-known and successful coaching inn in the town, a stage on the London-Manchester coach road, the depot for mail coaches, and praised even by the hyper-critical Viscount Torrington. In 1790, he was pleased to be charged two shillings and ninepence ha'penny for a meal of cold mutton, salad, tarts, and jellies with wine, rum and brandy to drink and hay and corn for his horse.

"A very good inn," he called it, but all that remains of it is a single fireplace and a mullioned window that used to light the loft where the postboys slept. In 1804, its owner, the Duke of Rutland, had it demolished, rebuilt, and renamed, as so often, after his good self. It pleased Jane Austen, who stayed here in 1811 and worked many local elements into a revision of her long-unpublished novel, *First Impressions*. Two years later – with Bakewell disguised as Lambton, and Chatsworth transmuted into Darcy's house, Pemberly – *First Impressions* was finally published with a new title, *Pride & Prejudice*.

The tenant for most of the 19th century, William Greaves, was a notable figure in the district, secretary of the High Peak Hunt for many years and, as late as 1862, proprietor of daily coach services to Rowsley, Whaley Bridge, Buxton, and Sheffield.

The Rutland's main claim to fame is as the birthplace of Bakewell Tart. It's not a tart but a pudding of pastry, beaten egg, and strawberry jam. The tale that it started out as a mistake on the part of Greaves's cook is surely rubbish. Cooks good enough to work in such a prominent inn shouldn't make such mistakes. But they do know their materials well enough to experiment deliberately and, in this case, triumphantly.

Above The current, rather stern square building was erected in 1804.

DEVON

OXENHAM ARMS
SOUTH ZEAL

A noble Tudor facade with stone porch and mullions conceals a much older building, for the Oxenham Arms was originally a canonry or lay monastery, built in the late 12th century.

One feature of the pub, however, is older still – older, indeed, than Christianity itself. For when the canons came to build their new home, they found that a megalith on the site, put there as long ago as 3000 BC, was too deep-set to budge, so they simply built their monastery around it. And there it remains to this day, a prehistoric standing stone forming part of the structure of a building more than 4,000 years its junior. Recent attempts to probe the inn's foundations have been abandoned at 20ft.

The great megalith is not the only huge piece of unworked stone in the pub. The mantelpiece of one fireplace is supported on a great upright splinter of granite, while the lintel of another is a slab 8ft long, 2ft deep, and of incalculable weight.

Its claim to have been an inn since 1477 is surely mistaken: it was still a canonry at the time of the Dissolution, when it was bought by the Burgoyne family. They, in turn, sold it to the Oxenhams, whose family legend features in Charles Kingsley's *Westward Ho!* It probably became an inn when they moved on to a grander dwelling and still retains the air of a home to the country gentry.

South Zeal and its inn feature large in two novels: Sabine Baring-Gould's *John Herring* and Eden Phillpotts' *The Beacon*, whose heroine Elizabeth Densham arrives in the village as the Oxenham's new barmaid. Phillpotts called the inn "the stateliest and most ancient abode in the hamlet" and, indeed, it is a fine building that would merit attention even without its megalithic curio.

Left The Tudor facade fronts a 12th-century structure.

DORSET

GROSVENOR
SHAFTESBURY

When Shaftesbury Abbey surrendered to Henry VIII's commissioners in 1540, it was already over 700 years old, and the guest-house belonging to it, which evolved into today's Grosvenor, may have been equally ancient.

However, by the time of the Dissolution, the guest-house seems already to have parted company with its parent, for we find a mention of it in 1533, operating as the New Inn. By 1626, it had become the Red Lion and, in the 18th century, it became the town's principal inn, attracting the bulk of the coach trade using a road to the West Country originally laid out by King Alfred in 882 – now, prosaically, the A30. From 1785-1822, the local quarter sessions were held in a specially constructed hall at the back of the inn.

In 1826, the owner, the Duke of Westminster, decided on a major rebuilding. What, if anything, survived of the Saxon work was now utterly swept away and replaced by the existing building, with a large, well-proportioned assembly room, and bearing its owner's surname. Even after the last coach had departed, the Grosvenor flourished. In 1878, it bought and incorporated its neighbours, the Cock and the Star.

The Grosvenor is the proud possessor of a remarkable piece of Victorian furniture, the Chevy Chase sideboard, still to be seen in the old assembly room. It was commissioned by the Duke of Northumberland in 1857, and completed by the Newcastle-upon-Tyne carver Gerard Robinson in 1863. It is 12ft long and 10ft high and is covered with hundreds of carved wooden figurines in a diorama of the *Ballad of Chevy Chase*, which tells of the 14th-century battle of Otterburn between 1,500 Northumbrians led by Harry Percy – Hotspur of Shakespeare's *Henry IV* - and 2,000 Scots led by the Douglases.

According to the ballad, the conflict was provoked by Percy, who was allegedly poaching on Douglas lands. The battle was so fierce that only 53 Northumbrians and 55 Scots survived. Hotspur himself is shown on the diorama, dying after the battle in the arms of his wife – although, in fact, both he and Douglas survived to fight on the same (losing) side against Henry IV at Shrewsbury in 1402.

Above The Grosvenor is a neo-classical building.

Co. Durham

Ancient Unicorn
BOWES

Charles Dickens stayed here one January, while investigating Shaw's Academy, the model for Dotheboys Hall in *Nicholas Nickleby*. Even on a summer's day, one can imagine how bleak Bowes can be in mid-winter. It was made all the bleaker by what Dickens discovered about the Academy. A farmer in the bar of the Unicorn begged him not to trust any child to Shaw and, in the churchyard, he came upon the grave of George Ashton Taylor, a pupil of the Academy, who died aged 19 and who was, by the power of Dickens's imagination, immortalised as the pitiful Smike.

"The first gravestone I stumbled on on that dreary afternoon," wrote Dickens of his graveyard stroll, "stood over a boy who had died suddenly; I suppose his heart broke. He died in this wretched place, and I think his ghost put Smike into my mind." In the event, Dickens, who was pretending to check the Academy on behalf of a friend, never gained admission. Shaw was warned of his purpose and refused to see him. Dotheboys Hall and Wackford Squeer are, thus, true fictions.

As well as enjoying the posting trade on the Roman road, the Unicorn's landlords had a smallholding at the rear and were stintholders, or commoners, on the surrounding moors. The court that dealt with the management of the moors met here for generations.

The interior was ruined in the 1970s, when the owners ripped out the dividing walls to create the single bar popular at the time. The present owners are trying to restore the original plan of separate, cosy, intimate bars and snugs. To help them, the granddaughter of Greta Pickersgill, who was the last of many generations of Pickersgills to run the Unicorn, has supplied details of the old layout and, at time of writing, they are nerving themselves (and their bank manager) to start work.

Left The stark stone 17th-century front is daunting in its neo-classical severity.

MORRITT ARMS
GRETA BRIDGE

This handsome inn was, of course, the place where Charles Dickens and Hablot Browne took refuge from a blizzard on their tour of the area researching *Nicholas Nickleby* in 1838. There are cartoons of Dickens characters on the walls of the bar; there is a clock by Humphreys of Bowes (remember Master Humphrey's Clock?); the Dickens Society even meets here from time to time.

Only it wasn't. In the letter to his wife describing his journey, Dickens never names the inn where he and Browne took refuge, and the description he gives of it "standing alone in the middle of a dreary moor" hardly fits the Morritt Arms, which nestles in the wooded valley down which the little River Greta clatters over its stony bed on its way to meet the Tees.

In coaching days, Greta Bridge, being on the Roman road (the remains of a fort are visible beside the Tees, and in the 1920s, the fort's vicus, or civilian settlement, was unearthed where the Morritt Arms now stands) and a convenient distance from Carlisle, was a prominent overnight stop on the London-Carlisle route with more than one inn. Dickens's letter better describes Thorpe Grange nearby, then the New Inn, although Browne's illustration appears to show the George just across the bridge – an inn no more, alas. It is even said that the Morritt Arms was not an inn at all at the time, but the seat of the important local family after which it is named. Even the cartoons turn out to have been painted in the 1940s by a local artist with a large bar-bill to settle.

Do not, however, allow any of this literary nonsense to spoil your pleasure. Dickens may never have spent the night here in a blizzard, but it's the sort of place where being benighted in a blizzard would be good. It has an expansive, well-heeled, tasteful yet informal atmosphere and is deservedly popular with locals and with trippers both British and international.

Previous page The Morritt Arms – a solid, ivy-clad inn with mature gardens.

Above It has the character of the Georgian squire's house it may well once have been.

ESSEX

SUN
DEDHAM

Architectural historian Niklaus Pevsner wrote, "Nothing in Dedham offends the eye" – but he was guilty of understatement. For everything in Dedham delights the eye: the elegant brick-fronted Georgian houses, those half-timbered frontages that escaped the addition of classical facades, the noble 14th-century church with its massive flint tower.

This is the very heart of Constable country, the rich and rolling Stour Valley where the artist who is to many England's greatest painter was born and nurtured, and where he returned throughout his life.

Born in 1776, the son of a miller, he was schooled in Dedham and encouraged in his art by local worthies. Many of his most important works were studies of local sites: the River Stour, the Vale of Dedham and St Mary's tower. Flatford, where both *Flatford Mill* and *The Haywain* were painted, is just a mile away.

Opposite the churchyard, and shaded by a massive chestnut, is the Sun, already 200 years old when Constable knew it. Once a coaching inn on the London-Norwich road, its 16th-century front is concealed behind the obligatory plastered facade. An unusual feature is the exceptionally tall coach arch: it looks as if the inn had taken over a neighbouring cottage and roofed over the lane between. The old coach office on one side of the arch is now an antiques shop.

Through the arch, one finds that the yard, where once sweating coach-horses steamed and stamped and ostlers bustled, is now a huge garden. Harper, visiting in 1903, wrote: "It is remarkable what picturesqueness lingers in the courtyards of old inns. The front of the house may have been modernised or in some way smartened up, but the old gables and casement windows are still generally to be found in the

rear; and sometimes the church tower comes in across the roof tops in a partly benedictory and wholly sketchable way, as at the village of Dedham, where the yard of the Sun and the church tower combine to make a very fine composition."

When Harper visited, the Sun's great days seemed to be behind it for, with no coach trade, it had become little more than a village beer-house. Now, with the gentrification of the area and the influx of tourists drawn by its association with Constable, the great days are back.

Above The classical front and sash windows date from Constable's era.

Above The Bell was built in the 15th century to lodge passing merchants.

BELL
HORNDON-ON-THE-HILL

South Essex is not noted for its villages and ancient inns. But, in a green gap between Basildon, Brentwood, Upminster, and Stanford-le-Hope, lies Horndon-on-the-Hill and the 500-year-old Bell.

In the Middle Ages, the village was a place of some importance, standing at the crossroads of an east-west route between London and the ports of Mucking and Fobbing and a north-south route connecting the wool-rich regions of central East Anglia with the ferry across the Thames at Tilbury and thence the Channel ports. It was also the centre of a woollen district.

There are signs that the timbers of the inn's armature are older than the building itself. The practice of reusing ship's timbers – cheaper than new oak, and pickled iron-hard by seawater – was common wherever they were available.

The Bell flourished in Tudor times, though the Marian persecution left a nasty blot, when a local landowner who refused to revert to Papism was burnt at the stake in the yard. Putting this ugly episode behind it, the Bell became both posting-house and village alehouse.

The Bell sweated out the 19th century as a picturesque local. That development in this quiet corner was slow is demonstrated by the fact that when the Bonson family took over in 1938, there was still no electricity, and water came from the yard pump.

During the Second World War, Mrs Bonson drove the village taxi and was charged with distributing the villagers' gas-masks. Mr Bonson became the fire-chief, as he had the only vehicle in the village that could tow the pump. The Bell had 40 soldiers billeted on it and put up bombed-out villagers. The local Home Guard drilled in the yard.

The inn is now run by the Bonsons' daughter Christine and her husband John Vereker, who have also converted Hill House, two doors down, into a 10-bedroom hotel and restaurant. The Bell is famous for its food and wine and wins award after award.

BLUE BOAR
MALDON

One of the worst things about East Anglia is its yellow brick. Sadly, that's what was used to build the late Georgian front of the Blue Boar at Maldon. But beauty is only skin-deep – and, in this case, the lack of it is only brick-deep.

Maldon stands at the head of the Blackwater, a prime invasion route, and one used by the Viking army of Olaf Trygvasson in 991. By this time, as far as the English were concerned, Viking invasions were ancient history, the Danes having been thrashed by King Alfred a century before; so the raid took the local earl, Byrtnoth, completely by surprise. On a narrow causeway at Maldon, which you can still see, he duly gave battle and was killed, his heroic death inspiring an epic poem, *The Battle Of Maldon*, of an emotional intensity and dramatic power which the passage of a millennium has done nothing to dim.

In the later Middle Ages, Maldon became a manor of the de Veres, earls of Oxford but very powerful in East Anglia. The Blue Boar, standing at the top of the hill, down whose seaward slope Maldon's high street straggles, was the centre of the manor and may even have been a de Vere residence before becoming an inn, possibly in the 14th century.

Having got beyond that brick front via the coaching arch, one finds oneself in an attractive and atmospheric medieval inn-yard. On the right are the elegant Georgian apartments – a fine dining-room, an understated lounge – while to the left are the tap-room and, behind it, a second bar, with beer drawn straight from the cask, in a higgledy-piggledy half-timbered 600-year-old stable-block. An exposed section of wattle and daub shows its primitive but durable form of construction.

Before you leave the Blue Boar yard, look over the inn roof at the steeple across the road. At All Saints, Christopher Jones, captain of the *Mayflower*, was christened and Laurence Washington, ancestor of George Washington, was buried. Look more closely and you'll see something else: it has England's only triangular church tower.

Above The Blue Boar's name comes from the de Vere family coat of arms.

GLOUCESTERSHIRE

NOEL ARMS
CHIPPING CAMPDEN

The narrow wooded valleys, unspoilt villages and towns, and honey-gold local stone of the Cotswolds all tell the English a story about themselves that they like to hear.

Chipping Campden is one of those Cotswold towns where auctioneers and solicitors, confident and comfortable in tweed and twill, rub cold shoulders with genteel but anxious secondhand booksellers whose capital is all tied up in a highly seasonal trade and who secretly rather regret the villa in Wimbledon and the foregone salary.

The Noel Arms spans both these worlds. The Campden & District Historical & Archaeological Society's history of local inns reveals that, in the 1780s, the Noel Arms (then the George) witnessed many legal consultations and transactions. You rather suspect that an awful lot of decisions are now, as then, stitched up here, well ahead of any publicly-scrutinised meeting.

The inn's atmosphere and nouveau-ish menu are perfectly calculated to attract both the dollar-rich heritage-trail tourists, who tramp the streets of this ancient market town, and the arts and craftsfolk who, oh so tastefully, prey on them.

The reality of towns like Chipping Campden and inns like the Noel Arms is enough to cure all but the most advanced cases of cynicism. The truth is that it's a beautiful pub in a beautiful town, where you can easily visualise convoys of pack-ponies with their loads of wool lining up in the lane behind the inn, ready to depart for Bristol and the sea. You can imagine the functions in the Assembly Room and the commercials, having been ferried up from the station by the inn's own omnibus, booking the brougham wherewith to complete the morrow's round of calls. Can't you?

Above The Georgian ashlar front and Victorian gothic annexe have an air of solidity.

Above The tiered galleries survive from the inn's coaching heyday.

NEW INN
GLOUCESTER

Of England's 18 medieval kings, eight met violent ends. Edward II, murdered at Berkeley Castle in September 1327, undoubtedly met the nastiest of them. Sodomising him with a red-hot wire was intended to discredit as well as kill him. Nevertheless, as soon as he was buried in Gloucester Abbey, his tomb became a focus for pilgrimage; for it was believed that the person of a king was sacred, so his body must have miraculous powers.

The New Inn was one of many guest-houses and hospices founded to lodge these pilgrims. It was designed and built in 1445 by a monk of the abbey, John Twyning, and is renowned for its galleried courtyard, which is easily the largest and most impressive of the handful of survivals.

The first-floor open gallery surrounds all four sides of the courtyard, and many of the bedrooms open off it, as they have always done, giving today's guests a chance to recapture at least something of the flavour of coaching days and earlier. A second tier was probably enclosed in Georgian times.

A yard of this size was such a convenient place of assembly that it quickly became a central place in the life of the town. In Tudor times, plays were performed here by companies of strolling actors –

Above The building's facade was renovated in the 18th century.

89

Shakespeare himself may have been one of them. On 9 July 1552, tradition has it, the Earl of Northumberland proclaimed his daughter-in-law, Lady Jane Grey, queen here in the short-lived Protestant coup which gave us the expression "nine days' wonder".

In the 18th century, the New Inn became an important coaching inn. New chimneys, doorcases, and windows were put in, and the first-floor residents' lounge appears to have been used as a small assembly room or a large private parlour.

When coaching declined, so did the New Inn: the coach office became the railway parcel office, the dining-room was let out as a Sunday School; and Harper, writing in 1903, mentions the "neglect and decay of 70 years ago." But by his time, motorists, commercial travellers, and tourists (not all of them car-borne: the inn still had an ostler!) had led to a revival in the inn's fortunes: "Most ancient inns of this character are merely poor survivals, archeologically interesting but wan veterans tottering to decay and long deserted by custom," he wrote. "Here, however, there is heavy traffic down in the yard; the ostler is busy; bells are ringing and luggage coming and going; appetising scents come from glowing kitchens, and to and from private rooms are carried trays of as good things as ever pilgrims feasted upon."

It has had more ups and downs since, including a long stint as a Berni Inn, but a recent restoration by a more sympathetic owner has made a true inn of it again.

WHITE HART ROYAL
MORETON-IN-MARSH

"Moreton-in-Marsh, where the frogs croak harsh," goes the rhyme, alluding to the swampy nature of the area and the town's name. It has been argued that the name derives from the town's marcher position – the Four Shires stone stood at the conjunction of Gloucestershire, Oxfordshire, Warwickshire, and Worcestershire until the county boundaries were changed. But the fact that it was called Moreton Henmarsh until a couple of centuries ago and was notoriously apt to flood, until the area was drained, rather confirms the simpler explanation.

Above The reception area's cobbled floor shows it was once the coach arch.

A neat stone-built town with good inns for travellers, Celia Fiennes called Moreton in the 1690s; and, indeed, its inns always had plenty of custom. The town stands at the junction of the Fosse Way and the London-Worcester road, and became a major trading centre, with a weekly market and a six-day fair in September, as early as the 13th century.

During the Civil War, the garrisons of both sides supplied themselves by extortion and robbery. The whole royal army passed through Moreton once, in July 1644, and Charles I confirmed the White Hart's status as principal inn by billeting himself in it.

By that time, the White Hart was probably about a century old: moulded beams and a great Tudor fireplace were discovered during restoration work 100 years ago. A 17th-century print shows a carved gantry sign spanning the street.

The London-Worcester road was turnpiked in 1731, and the Fosse Way in 1755. The improvements to the roads hastened the growth of coach services through the town, which was a staging post on the 113-mile London-Worcester service. The White Hart shared the coach trade with at least four other inns.

A railway line to Stratford was built in 1826, used by horse-drawn goods wagons to haul wool to Stratford and coal and other bulk commodities back to Moreton, undercutting the canal barges, which had previously handled the traffic. But, even when the local line was taken over and incorporated into the main line, it did the White Hart no harm. It is listed as a commercial and posting inn in a directory of 1870, showing that the railway could create trade as well as destroy it.

Left The neo-classical front was acquired in the late 1700s.

CROSS HANDS
OLD SODBURY

The Cross Hands is an enormous place to find in the middle of nowhere; but to a mail-coach operator it was the ideal location – on a crossroads, and the right distance from Bath to the south and Bristol to the west to make the first change of horses.

The present 18th-century inn stands on 14th-century foundations; its cellars were reputedly used as a holding tank for prisoners in the wake of Monmouth's rebellion of 1685. Its size – it is a surprise to find that it has only 24 bedrooms – and its architecture testify to the great success of its location.

The most interesting thing about it is its name, and the story advanced to explain it. Supposedly, a coin minted by the Roman dictator Marius in 102 BC, depicting clasped hands as a symbol of unity with the legend *concordia militum*, was fished out of a well, and it was decided to use the symbol as the inn's trademark.

Now then. Who fished it out of the well, and when? And why rename the inn – for if there was a well, there must already have been an inn? And how did the coin – struck 150 years before the Roman invasion of Britain – get down the well in the first place? It certainly didn't arrive in the wallet of a Roman soldier: who carries 150-year-old coins round with them? And was the well already there when the Romans arrived? … oh, I do love a good debunk!

Actually, the name may be rare but is not unique: there are at least three others, and the chances are that both name and symbol derive from some family's armorial bearings. But the Roman coin story was in circulation when Charles Harper arrived in 1903; at which time, the inn's location, once to its advantage, had turned against it.

"In a wooded hollow at the crossroads respectively to Chipping Sodbury and Chippenham," he wrote, "you come to the wholly deserted Plough inn and the half-deserted, rambling old coaching and posting-inn of Cross Hands, where a mysterious sign, unexplainable by

the innkeeper, hangs out, exhibiting two hands crossed, with squabby, spatulate fingers and the inscription *Caius Marius Imperator BC102 Concordia Militum*. What it all means passes the wit of man, or at any rate of local man, to discover."

Make what you will of the name: the inn's fortunes had definitely revived when the journalist and publisher Norman Tiptaft called in the late 1940s. It had been taken over by a former naval Lieutenant Commander and his wife, who brought in an experienced maitre d'hotel and two chefs, one French and one Swiss, to enliven the post-war gloom of this particular corner of Britain.

"The British and continental cuisine is deservedly famous, and the wine cellar is a revelation," he wrote – just as well, since the dining-room had to be cleared one day in 1981 to allow no less a person than the Queen to sit out a blizzard. She had tea and scones while she waited, but history does not record whether she paid for her afternoon tea in cash or plastic or, indeed, at all.

Above The rambling old coaching inn is conveniently placed between Bath and Bristol.

UNICORN
STOW-ON-THE-WOLD

Stow is often called the capital of the Cotswolds and, in the Unicorn, it is blessed with a capital Cotswold inn. Stow's main feature is its huge central square, now partly built over but still extensive. From 1107 until World War I, it was the scene of a weekly market, which was important in the town's early prosperity. As well as the market, there were travellers on the Fosse Way to cater for and, in 1476, Edward IV chartered two annual fairs, which drew merchants from as far afield as Flanders and northern Italy.

All this economic activity meant plenty of business for the town's inns, which, at the time, included the Talbot, the King's Arms, the White Hart, the Queen's Head, the Red Lion, and the Unicorn. The dislocation caused by the Thirty Years' War in the 17th century, saw a sharp downturn, which was worsened by the English Civil War.

In March 1646, Stow was the scene of the last pitched battle of the war. Sir Jacob Astley was attempting to relieve Oxford with 3,000 men, when he was ambushed by a superior Parliamentary force. After a long resistance, his force broke; the wounded were massacred; the streets ran with blood; and 1,000 prisoners were crammed into the church.

The following century saw a revival in Stow's fortunes, boosted by the turnpiking of the local roads in 1755. Dozens of regular coach services were established, as were many carriers, liveries, and posting businesses. There was even an attempt, in the 18th century, to establish a spa.

As well as the coach trade, the Unicorn also possessed a big tract of ground, which was developed as something approaching a pleasure garden, where archery, football, bowls, quoits, and cricket were played. Given that post-match refreshments were commonly on a heroic scale, it was a useful boost for business.

The Unicorn's handsome neo-classical front looks south down the Fosse Way, and the carriage arch is, unusually, sited in the side of the building, in the middle of a long range of stables.

Left The Unicorn was extensively rebuilt in 1755.

BELL

TEWKESBURY

The beautiful half-timbered Bell stands just across the street from Tewkesbury's magnificent abbey church, on the site of the monastery guest-house.

After the Dissolution, the old guest-house was briefly a tannery, but was entirely rebuilt as the Angel Inn in the late 16th or early 17th century. The date, 1697, above the door applies to a rebuilding for, in the dining-room, there are traces of a wall-painting, which is probably Elizabethan. Some of the interior wooden panelling may have come from the old monastery.

In the 18th century, the Bell shared the coach trade with the Hop Pole – an inn used by Charles Dickens as a setting for episodes in *The Pickwick Papers*. But in 1857, the Bell gained the upper hand over the Hop Pole in the battle of literary associations and even became something of a tourist attraction, when Mrs Craik made it the model for the home of Abel Fletcher in her best-seller *John Halifax, Gentleman*.

Mrs Craik – the pseudonym of Dinah Mulock – got the idea for the book on a visit to the abbey in 1852, and ransacked Tewkesbury for further details. A gravestone supplied the name for her hero. Lunch at the Bell inspired her to make it the pivot of the story. The landlord said it had once been the home of a tanner; so Abel Fletcher's trade was decided. The Bell became a place of pilgrimage for fans, especially Americans and, when Mrs Craik died 30 years later, she was given a monument in the abbey. But, as well as its transient literary fame, the Bell enjoyed a more securely rooted place in local social life. Until the regatta was wound up in 1921, the Bell was always the scene of the town's regatta ball.

Above The timber-framed inn is one of many Tudor buildings in the town.

HAMPSHIRE

SHIP & BELL
HORNDEAN

Horndean may have been too insignificant in coaching days even to be marked in *Pigot's County Atlas*, but the Ship & Bell should loom large in any atlas of ale. For the town, and particularly the inn, are home to one of Britain's finest country breweries.

Horndean in the 17th century was a mere hamlet in the parish of Catherington. But its position astride the London-Portsmouth road, a convenient stage from Portsmouth, guaranteed its inn a healthy posting trade, its popularity doubtless enhanced by its rather self-consciously nautical name.

In 1847, when coaching and posting were moribund, the inn was bought by the local coal and corn merchant Richard Gale, whose family had been grocers and bakers in Horndean for a century.

The Ship & Bell already had a reputation for the quality of its own-brewed ale. When Richard's son George Alexander Gale took over the running of the inn in 1853, he decided to expand the brewing side of the business. This was a step many other innkeeper-brewers were also taking. Thirteen of the country's surviving regional breweries were either founded or expanded from a home-brew operation into a full-blown commercial brewery between 1838 and 1858.

Steam technology lay behind the boom. It allowed raw materials and finished goods to be transported economically; it enabled big breweries to produce larger volumes of more consistent beer more cheaply than pub-breweries could; and it created the cities that became the market for the first industrially-produced beers.

In 1869, the brewery behind the Ship & Bell burnt down, and George Alexander built a new brewery next door. The Ship & Bell became the brewery tap and, while Gale's continued to expand, taking over other local breweries such as Homewell's of Havant and the Angel Brewery of Midhurst, the inn continued to serve its beers at their peak of perfection.

If you find yourself dining there, and are lucky enough not to be driving, then, instead of port or Cognac as your digestif, try a bottle of Gale's Prize Old, a rich, vinous ale of nine per cent alcohol, served in a high-shouldered 18th-century bottle with a driven cork. And as you sip, reflect how appropriate it is that the surrounding area is known as the Forest of Bere.

Above In the mid-18th century, the inn was given the obligatory neo-classical facade.

WHITE HORSE
ROMSEY

The grand, handsome Georgian-fronted White Horse, which stands opposite the Norman abbey in Romsey's market square, is as perfect a type of the English coaching inn as you could hope to find.

It is thought that the first building on the site was an abbey guest-house in the 12th century; and although much of the interior is Elizabethan – including remnants of typical Tudor wall-paintings uncovered during restoration in 1962 – it is believed that a good deal of the fabric, including the cellars, is early medieval. (The tale of a tunnel linking inn and abbey, by the way, looks unlikely, as an underground stream flows down the street between them.)

Romsey lies at the centre of a whole knot of main roads linking Southampton, London, Portsmouth, and Salisbury, and is about seven miles – or one short stage – north of Southampton docks. With a location like that, it is hardly surprising that the town's inns flourished even before the coaching trade really hit its stride, and the White Horse was the first among them.

In 1776, the inn had 35 bedrooms, six public rooms, stabling for 50 horses, and a coach-house for four carriages. As well as travellers, it catered for local needs too: there was a cockpit under today's bar. At that time, it was run by a couple called Sibley, who seemed to have a particularly hard streak about them. Two of their employees had to apply for poor relief, one saying his wages were only 30/- a year, a second claiming not to have been paid for 20 years!

The present facade probably dates from 1811, when the Paving Commission was offering subsidies for the "tidying-up" of older frontages, especially those with jettied upper floors or projecting porches. (The inn's owners were also subsidised to maintain a street-light.) It may also have been at this time that the open galleries evident in the yard were closed in.

Left The white, stuccoed, neo-classical front belies the inn's age.

DOLPHIN
SOUTHAMPTON

The awesome classical facade of the Dolphin conceals foundations some 600 years older, for the first record of a building on the site was in 1200, when a couple called Simon and Celia paid 8s a year rent for it. By 1220, it was two dwellings, one of them probably an alehouse. By 1454, when the name *le Dolphyn* was first recorded, it had become one large house belonging to William Gunter, a wealthy merchant and local mayor. By 1506, the Dolphin had become a prominent inn, and buildings at the rear are of 16th-century origin. In 1588, the landlord, Edward Wilmot, became an MP, and one of his successors, John Jefferies, was knighted by James I.

Even before the first public coach services, the Dolphin's location near the harbour in the leading port of the south coast had attracted a fair number of prominent guests: Sir Humphrey Gilbert, explorer of the New World, in 1582; the Moroccan Ambassador in 1635; and Charles I himself, in 1646. But in the age of coaching – and one of the earliest mail coaches ran from the Dolphin to the Swan With Two Necks in Lad Lane, London – such visits became the rule rather than the exception. The Dolphin became Southampton's, and one of England's, most important termini.

A magnificent ballroom was added in 1785, and a newly-discovered moulded plaster ceiling, in what is now the County Room, originally graced one of many private parlours for very, very distinguished guests. Among them were William IV; Thackeray, who wrote much of *Pendennis* at the hotel; and Jane Austen, who lived in Southampton between 1807 and 1809 and was a regular at the Dolphin's subscription balls. In a letter to her sister Cassandra, she wrote of a black-eyed French officer with whom she danced, but whom she found disappointing.

The collapse of coaching made no difference to business, since the railway and the docks still brought wealthy travellers who required luxury – among them, Queen Victoria en route for Osborne, whose coach-horses were customarily stabled at the Dolphin to await her return from the Isle of Wight. In the early part of World War One, the inn's location and facilities made it an ideal choice as the HQ for the British Expeditionary Force.

Above The present inn, completed in 1760, has the country's largest bow-windows.

HEREFORDSHIRE

GREEN DRAGON
HEREFORD

Originally named the White Lion, the ancient city of Hereford's oldest inn did a quick *volte-face* when Henry VII toppled the Yorkist dynasty at Bosworth in 1485.

The White Lion, according to tradition, is where Owen Tudor, leader of the local Lancastrians, and other prisoners were held the night after the Yorkist victory of Mortimer's Cross in February 1461, to be beheaded in the market-place next morning by the young Earl of March, soon to be Edward IV and "this glorious son of York".

Owen had married Queen Katherine of France, Henry V's widow and Henry VI's mother, so he was a prominent Lancastrian nationally as well as locally. But, according to Gregory's *Chronicle*, he had not fully realised the price of failure in national politics at the time:

"All the way to the scaffold he had not believed that he would be beheaded till he saw the axe and the block and the collar of his red velvet doublet was ripped off. Then he said: 'That head shall lie on the stock that was wont to lie on Queen Katherine's lap,' and he put his heart and mind wholly unto God, and full meekly took his death."

Afterwards, says the *Chronicle*: "His head was set upon the top step of the market cross, and a mad woman combed his hair and washed the blood from his face, and she got candles and placed them about him, and lit them, more than a hundred of them."

Owen, as it happens, was Henry VII's grandfather; Jasper Tudor, Earl of Pembroke, was Henry's uncle, and his arms included a green dragon. For Hereford's leading inn to adopt it as its sign was a clear show of submission on the part of a city that had played host to the Yorkists' crime – and which, perhaps more to the point, was located deep in Yorkist territory.

By the time Owen Tudor breathed his last, the inn was already two or three centuries old. Its owners claim an 11th-century origin for it, although on what evidence they do not say. Tudor displeasure evidently did it no harm for, with its size, age, and location it flourished mightily. As one of the few crossings over the Wye, Hereford was the centre of a tangle of long-distance routes, and you only have to look at the Green Dragon's magnificent Georgian frontage to see how completely it came to dominate the town's coach trade.

The city's economic dominance of a wealthy, but sparsely-populated region ensured the Green Dragon's survival of the advent of rail pretty much unscathed as the county's pre-eminent social and business centre.

Above The 25 bays give the inn an almost Palladian appearance.

Above The 16th-century front has been tidied up, but not completely replaced.

FEATHERS
LEDBURY

Thickly wooded Herefordshire is famous for its half-timbered buildings, and the small but exquisite market town of Ledbury – native town of the medieval poet Langland and his more recent successors Elizabeth Barrett and John Masefield – is generously sprinkled with them. The Market House, the Tudor House (once the King's Arms), and the House on Props are all splendid examples of 16th-century timber framing, as is the Feathers.

Built in 1565, the Feathers became the town's principal inn when the era of coaching dawned and it was found that the carriage arch at the previously dominant King's Arms – despite its generous stabling and banquet hall – was simply too narrow for full-sized coaches. In 1778, it went to the wall.

As the town's main coaching inn, the Feathers continued to expand and, in 1784, when mail coaches superseded post-boys, it became a station on the Aberystwyth-Cheltenham route. At about that time, the old casements were replaced with sashes, but no other permanent changes were made to the front. It was, in fact, plastered over to achieve the regularity and symmetry favoured at the time, without going to the expense of adding a completely new frontage. In addition, a Georgian wing was added at the back, complete with an assembly room built on pillars over the yard. At the same time, a Tudor house next door was incorporated as part of the inn.

The Feathers' coach trade lasted well into the 19th century, when the stables also housed the many private vehicles owned by country gentry visiting the town. For two centuries, a box-pew was reserved in the town's huge parish church for guests who did not take travelling as an excuse for missing divine service.

HERTFORDSHIRE

SUN
HITCHIN

Hitchin has been an important town since before the Conquest – as a market, a river-crossing, the site of a large and wealthy abbey, and the centre of a rich grain-growing district, renowned for the quality of its malt.

The Sun is first recorded in 1575 and probably stood here 50 years earlier. However, it only rose to prominence in 1741, when a local family called Kershaw set up a posting service between Hitchin and London, the Hitchin end of the line being the Sun Inn's yard. This was not an uncommon arrangement and, in this case, lasted for more than a century.

Coach travel brought with it the risk of robbery, but the highwaymen of the time did not confine their activities to the road. In 1772, three of them held up the Sun at gunpoint, robbing and binding the landlord, William Marshall, and his guests and, before making off with their plunder, scratching their initials and the date on the brickwork by the door.

By this time, the front of the inn had already been rebuilt in neo-classical style. But the builders left an interesting legacy, in

110

Above The rambling Tudor work has given way to the more disciplined Georgian style.

the form of a "secret chamber" at the junction of the old work and the new, with access apparently through a cupboard. Again, this is not unusual and can have a number of reasons. It might have been a privy; it might have been a bedroom for the servants or children of the guests in the main room; or it might simply have been an awkward corner, walled off and forgotten, as often occurred.

As well as being a substantial coaching inn on the London-Leeds route, the Sun played its part in the life of the town. The petty sessions met here; the town's fire engine was based in the yard; the Hitchin Loyal Volunteers had their HQ here; and the Sun even doubled as Town Hall until one was built in 1840. There was also a well-used Assembly Room, added in 1770.

The Kershaws wound up their coach service on 10 August 1850, three days after the first steam train had pulled into Hitchin's new railway station. But that wasn't the end of coaching at the Sun. The inn's owners continued to run a service into London for an incredible 30 years, hedging their bets, by running a horse-bus service to and from the station as well.

The famous local malt – finer than Spanish grapes for making liquor, Elizabeth I apparently said to the Spanish ambassador – found good use here. The Sun Inn operated its own maltings and brewhouse until after the Second World War.

WHITE HART
ST ALBANS

It's tragic to walk through the knot of streets around the great flint-built Abbey of St Albans and spy out the traces of its galaxy of long-gone coaching inns. The rows of shop-fronts are pierced by great arches, which are manifestly old coach arches. Through them, one glimpses yards, which are manifestly old inn-yards; and whose very names – Dolphin Yard, Half Moon Yard – are manifestly the names of vanished coaching inns.

St Albans in the coaching era was the first change of horses after the Holyhead road parted from the Great North Road at Barnet, and Holywell Hill was once a row of inns. Today, only the Peahen and the White Hart survive of the Old Crown, Saracens Head, Angel, Horsehead, Dolphin, Seven Stars, Woolpack, and Keys. Only the White Hart survives in anything like its original state, since the Peahen, built in 1556, was torn down and rebuilt in late Victorian times.

Above The neo-classical facade was removed in 1935 to reveal the old timber frames.

The White Hart has stood directly opposite Sumpter's Yard, which cuts through to the Abbey itself, since about 1470. So, it is more than likely that it will have put up its share of pilgrims, albeit under its original name, the Hartshorn. But in the later 17th century, it was transformed. The open galleries were filled in in 1660, when the existing narrow staircase with its characteristic short flights and barley-sugar-twist balustrade was built and the rude Tudor frescoes, partially uncovered by recent restorations, were plastered over. In 1690, the two-storey block containing the restaurant was added to the original building. The panelling in this area looks original, and is among the finest to be seen in any inn.

Above The front bars have a view of the Abbey's Norman tower.

Probably at about this time, the half-timbered front was stuccoed over and the casements replaced by neo-classical sashes. A primitive painting of the arrival of Simon Fraser, Lord Lovat, here in 1746, shows the inn front as having been appropriately modernised. (Lovat, a Jacobite captured after Culloden in 1745, was executed at the Tower in 1747. During a break in his journey at St Albans, he was sketched by Hogarth.)

The White Hart was the actual scene, during the coaching era, of a wonderfully gruesome accident used by Dickens in the *Pickwick Papers*, but relocated to the Golden Cross in London and recounted thus by Mr Jingle: "Other day – five children – mother, tall lady, eating sandwiches – forgot the arch – crash – children look round – mother's head off – sandwich in her hand – no mouth to put it in – head of a family off – shocking! shocking!"

The White Hart survived the demise of coaching, probably because it was further down Holywell Hill than the other inns and was, therefore, a less desirable redevelopment prospect. Just as well: Sir Albert Richardson in *The Old Inns Of England* said: "The remains of the great timber inns at St Albans, as in the old wing of the White Hart, show once again the inns of the cathedral cities and abbey towns to have been buildings of the first rank." In 1935, the year after his great work was published, the White Hart was restored and the two front bars were panelled. Sir Albert would have certainly approved.

Above Most of the panelling was replaced this century, but here it is probably original.

KENT

FALSTAFF
CANTERBURY

The date given for the foundation of this venerable inn is invariably 1403, which, given that its original name was the White Hart, would have made its first landlord a very brave man indeed. For the White Hart was the badge of Richard II, murdered in the Lancastrian coup of 1399, and Henry IV might not have been over-pleased at such open adherence to the legitimate line.

Whether the inn is a little older or a little younger than its given date, it contains much fine 15th-century work, including linenfold panelling, huge fireplaces, and oak beams so hardened by age that German bombs failed to set them alight when the Falstaff was hit in 1940.

The location is a great point of interest. Canterbury at that time, as we know from Chaucer, was a huge centre of pilgrimage – easily the greatest in England, and one of the greatest in Europe. Inside the city, clustered more than 20 religious houses of various sorts and sizes, and every one had at least one guest-house, maybe more, to lodge the thousands of pilgrims who flocked to the shrine of Thomas Beckett.

There were also many inns grouped round the Westgate, supposedly to lodge pilgrims who arrived after curfew and were too late to be admitted to the city itself. But those who put forward this explanation forget one important thing. Of course, late-coming pilgrims would have been glad of an open inn; but the essence of it is that the city's writ stopped at the gate, and inns just outside were free of all sorts of tolls, tithes, and taxes as well as irksome regulation. This quarter bore the same relationship to Canterbury as Southwark did to London: a tax-free red-light district – surely very welcome to the citizens of a virtual theocracy.

The White Hart's name was changed to the Falstaff in 1783.

Above The inn originally had a gallows sign that spanned the street.

ROYAL VICTORIA & BULL
ROCHESTER

"Good house, nice beds," said Mr Jingle of the Bull, the principal inn of the ancient cathedral city of Rochester. This was a loaded remark because it was made by a fictitious character about a genuine inn. According to Richardson, the Bull had been designed "frankly as a public building in the solid Doric, Ionic or Corinthian of the time" just when "the snug English tradition of home from home was fast fading". It was the first stop on the Pickwickians' long journey into

Above The carriage arch still dominates the front of the building.

immortality, and the confusion between reality and fiction has persisted in people's minds ever since.

Although the visit of Pickwick, Tupman, Winkle and Snodgrass was set in 1827, it was actually written in 1836, in which year, Princess Victoria and her insufferable mother were detained here by bad weather. Next year, Victoria was Queen, and the inn's name was hastily changed to the Victoria & Bull, to extract the greatest possible advantage from the connection. The advantage evidently had a short shelf-life for, before long, the name was "Bull & Victoria" and, not long afterwards, it was the plain old Bull again.

It now announces itself as the Royal Victoria & Bull Hotel, and what that says about the waxing and waning of the currency of royal connections, I leave the reader to judge.

According to Harper, the Bull that Princess Victoria visited was the inn frequented by the "fine flower of Dockyard society with the even finer flower of the Garrison, wholly to the exclusion of the tradesfolk of Chatham, Rochester and Gillingham". But the Assembly Room, alas, no longer has that "elevated den" for musicians that Dickens describes and that Harper saw in 1926. Only its staircase survives. You will search the hall in vain for that "illustrious larder" of "noble joints and tarts" that Harper pronounced was more likely a china cabinet for, if the common practice of the times was any guide, the "very grove" of uncooked joints actually hung in the arch, where the current of air would dry and preserve it, not the hall, where warmth and moisture would hasten its decay.

But if the actualities of the Bull, which Dickens observed, have now mostly vanished, the fiction he made about it has survived, for Room 17 is still pointed out as Mr Pickwick's room.

"'So is this where Mr Pickwick is supposed to have slept?' remarked a visitor, when viewing bedroom 17 by favour of one of the inn's former landlords," recounts Harper. "The stranger meant no offence, but the landlord was greatly ruffled. 'Supposed to have slept? He did sleep here, sir!'"

LANCASHIRE

WHITE BULL
RIBCHESTER

The White Bull is a late Tudor or early 17th-century building but, as we so often find, the foundations on which it stands are very much older. In fact, the masonry in the cellars is reputed to be Roman, although it would take a proper dig to confirm it. But there might be something in it: in the summer of 1700, severe drought caused the level of the Ribble to sink, and many Roman remains were temporarily revealed. As many of these fragments as possible were recovered, and most found their way to museums.

But four complete Roman columns, said to be remains of a temple of Minerva, support the pub's porch, upon which the date of its construction, 1707, is carved.

For many years, the local magistrates used the White Bull as their courthouse. One room was used as a holding cell and, during redecorations, the rusting remains of a set of manacles were found embedded in the wall. Half a mile away is Gallows Lane and, until 1805, the bodies of those sent from the White Bull to Lancaster Crown Court for jury trial, and convicted and hanged in the county town, were returned here to be gibbeted as an example to their friends and relations.

The stables have room for only about six horses, showing that the inn never catered for much more than local traffic. A mounting-block of three very worn stone steps stands beside the front door.

Above and Right The crude wooden carving of a bull dates from the 18th century.

LEICESTERSHIRE

THREE SWANS
MARKET HARBOROUGH

The Three Swans was the third of the three inns to be owned by the self-proclaimed Pioneer Amateur Innkeeper John Fothergill, antiquarian, archaeologist, and artist. The first and most noted was the Spreadeagle at Thame near Oxford.

Fothergill turned to innkeeping in 1922, at the age of 46, having been on his way to academic celebrity before suffering a nervous breakdown during World War One. Whoever told him that innkeeping was a suitable career for a man of his temperament knew little either of the trade or of the man. If his copious writings are to be taken at face value, he spent the rest of his life in choleric battle against bilkers, bureaucrats, philistines, and people who used his lavatories without asking.

The Three Swans, when he took it over in the 1930s, was a faded coaching inn of early Tudor provenance, with a new front of about 1790. By the time of his arrival, it was so run-down as to be no more than a beerhouse; but, he said: "Whatever the dirt, the awful furniture and beds, the rat-holes, the wallpapers coming away from the walls, the tiny unventilated lavatory, you could see at once that the building itself had a loveable character."

Shortly after he and his wife Kate moved in, the loveable building virtually collapsed.

The Fothergills stayed at the Three Swans until 1952, when John retired, aged 77. Artistically, he did not repeat the success of the Spreadeagle, whose proximity to Oxford generated a clientele of a brilliance the stout East Midlanders could not hope to equal. But, as Fothergill found, Leicestershire folk were warmer than the yeomen of Thame. They took the notorious eccentric to their hearts – he had lain under the "foreigner ban" for his entire decade in Thame – and though

Right A new front was added to the Tudor building in about 1970.

122

they were puzzled by him, they were delighted by him too. The Birmingham journalist Norman Tiptaft, commenting on a lunch at the Three Swans, summed up a Fothergill curiosity in suitably blunt fashion: "I'd never eaten chutney with fish before. It's nice."

Fothergill's refusal to print a menu, because he didn't know what he was going to cook until he cooked it, was usually justified by the excellence of whatever he did, eventually, cook. His commitment to fresh ingredients would shame many modern hoteliers. He would tolerate only the best clientele, but he would have only the best for them.

"At the Spreadeagle," he wrote, "I chose and made a clientele to suit and refresh myself; here I decided to suit and refresh my clientele."

He got into some scrapes at the Three Swans, especially in the war: he fired half his staff at the outbreak in anticipation of reduced trade, only to find himself busier than ever because dining out was off the ration. He was arrested as a spy in Buxton for wearing a foreign-looking hat, and joined the Home Guard only after having had boots made on his own last, saying: "The certain agony of going in issue boots was the chief reason for having held back." A party of young women once asked him to tea, where he found they had been challenged to produce for their friends "the most original thing in Leicestershire". He is perhaps best summed up by an action of his own: "I once snatched a cigarette out of a man's mouth as he was drinking my claret!"

LINCOLNSHIRE

ANGEL & ROYAL
GRANTHAM

Simply the Angel until 1866, this is one of the most important inns, both culturally and historically, in the country. The site belonged to the Knights Templar until the order was suppressed in 1312, and there had been an inn on it for at least a century before that. King John and his retinue lodged in it in 1213, and there are traces of 12th- and 13th-century masonry in the cellar.

That John stayed at the inn has given rise to some fascinating speculation. Normally, and unlike later kings and queens, early

medieval monarchs would have lodged at a castle, especially in wartime; but Grantham has none. The layout and style of the front of the Angel & Royal, however, is reminiscent of a castle gatehouse, and one or two street-names suggest the existence of a castle. Add to that the fact that the inn stands at the highest point of the town, just where one would expect to find a castle, and the unsupported conclusion that the inn was really built as the gatehouse of a castle that was planned but never built has often been jumped to.

The oldest visible part of the building is its gateway, which dates back to the reign of Edward III (1327-77) who, with his queen, Phillipa of Hainault, adorns its hood mouldings. The rest of the frontage is

Above The walls at the front of the inn are unusually thick.

15th-century. The wall itself is a yard thick and may be contemporary with the gate, while the two bays, the small oriel over the gate with its carved angel, the parapet, and the buttresses are later embellishments.

The room behind the oriel is known as the *Chambre du Roi*, where Richard III, in October 1483, wrote to the Lord Chamberlain, instructing him to send the Great Seal wherewith to notarise a warrant for the execution of the Duke of Buckingham, hitherto his greatest supporter and the mastermind behind his coup earlier that year. Now a restaurant, this room is the hotel's showpiece. A copy of the letter is proudly displayed; the fan-vaulting in the oriel and the two bays is worth travelling to see.

On the ground floor, there are more examples of vaulting, two 14th-century fireplaces, and a carved pelican in piety feeding its young with its own blood – one of many religious symbols supporting the theory that this was a pilgrims' inn, serving the shrine of St Wulfram, to whom the parish church is dedicated.

After the Reformation, the inn continued to attract travellers – merchants, rather than pilgrims.

In 1706, the landlord, Michael Soloman, died, leaving £2 a year for a sermon to be preached every Michaelmas against drunkenness. In his day, the Great North Road saw its first coaches and, at its height, the Angel was a major halt for the York, Edinburgh & Aberdeen Mail; the Royal Charlotte, which plied between London and York; the York & Leeds Post Coach; and the York Highflyer. Viscount Torrington stopped by in 1791, at about the time that the old mullions were replaced by fashionable sashes and the two rather barrack-like rear ranges were added.

Left The gateway predates the other features on the front of the inn.

127

GEORGE
STAMFORD

An aristocrat of English inns, the George is one of more than 400 listed buildings in this old town. Soon after the Conquest, the site was granted to Peterborough Abbey and, in time, three ecclesiastical foundations were built on it. On the south side was the House of the Holy Sepulchre, a guest-house for pilgrims and crusaders en route to the Holy Land; a church stood where the garden is today; and on the north side an almshouse, the Hospital of St John and St Thomas, was built in 1174. All three properties were confirmed in the Abbey's possession by a charter of 1189.

Two centuries later, a chapel of St Mary Magdalene was added: apart from the crypt and chancel, it was completely destroyed in a Lancastrian raid and, shortly afterwards, the whole site was sold to a citizen called John Dickens, alderman in 1476, 1483, and 1493. His daughter Alice inherited the inn and married a townsman called David Cissell, one of Henry VII's sergeants-at-arms. Their son Richard was wealthy enough to buy the former Priory of St Martin's with 300 acres, and his son William was that chief minister of Elizabeth I's who built Burghley House on the edge of Stamford. He also had the whole George rebuilt, granting the tenant the right, exercised to this day, of nominating one inmate for the almshouses opposite.

In the days of coaching, the George's stock rose still further. Stamford was where the Great North Road crosses the Welland, which attracted a great volume of traffic. As principal inn, the George needed a separate tap for servants of wealthy travellers as early as 1714, in which year, the landlord was murdered by a Hessian dragoon as a suspected Jacobite.

Later in the century, when the George served 20 up and 20 down coaches a day, the front was rebuilt, and an Assembly Room, ballroom, minstrel's gallery, and gallows sign were added. There was also a cockpit 40ft across, with seating for 500. It was built in 1725 and, after cockfighting was abolished in 1849, it was converted into a school.

The landlord in the 18th century was wily enough to match his daughter to a future Bishop of London, the Rev Beilby Porteous. Royal guests have included Charles I, William III, the Duke of Cumberland, and the King of Denmark. Daniel Lambert, who died in 1809 weighing 52 stone 11lb, was a regular, as was novelist Sir Walter Scott.

Charles Harper declared, "There is an almost uncanny dignity about the George that makes you feel it is very kind to let you enter Stamford at all."

Above The 18th-century gallows sign still spans the road.

NORFOLK

DUKE'S HEAD
KING'S LYNN

Built, between 1685 and 1689, by a local architect who achieved a measure of national success, Henry Bell, the Duke's Head is a splendid classical building almost too fine to be an inn. In fact, it was not at first an ordinary inn at all. According to one account, it was actually built as a private mansion for a wealthy wine-shipper of Lynn, Sir John Turner, who also commissioned Bell to design the nearby Custom House, originally the Corn Exchange.

Another version has it that it was purpose-built as a guest-house for foreign merchants of consequence – on balance a likelier tale, as the Duke's Head stands on the site of a Tudor inn, the Griffin, whose staircase, with its turned baluster and oak rail, Bell incorporated into his new building.

Lynn was then the harbour serving a vast net of inland waterways, stretching to Bedford and beyond. A huge volume of goods passed through, and merchants from all over Europe spent lavishly, so the expense of building the Exchange and the inn was not entirely altruistic. Guests were feted with lavish banquets and balls, as befitted their importance to the city's economy. As a leading coaching inn in later years, the Duke's Head's exclusivity was jealously maintained. For many years, it denied admittance to anyone arriving on foot or even horseback – one was supposed to roll up in one's own carriage.

Occupying centre stage in local high society, the Duke's Head became the headquarters of the local masons in Victorian times, and entertained the Prince of Wales while he was staying at Sandringham and, doubtless, yearning to escape for a night on the town – even if the town was only King's Lynn.

Above The Duke's Head has a broad and imposing front.

MAIDS HEAD
NORWICH

This handsome inn with its "endlessly rambling corridors, many flights of stairs and a plan of tangled complexity designed for a game of hide and seek" (Sir Albert Richardson) stands on a site dripping with history.

In Norman times, a bishop's palace stood here, and Norman masonry is still visible in the cellar. It became an ecclesiastic hospice, and the Black Prince is reported to have lodged here while competing in a tournament. There appears to have been a tavern on or near the site in 1287, when a Robert the Fowler was convicted of theft, his address being given as "a tavern in Cook Row", which is identified with the site of the Maids Head. This tavern seems to have been called the Mold Fish or Murtel Fish Tavern, possibly a reference to the skate, a standby of the North Sea fisheries and known locally as an old maid.

The transition from tavern to inn had definitely occurred by 1472, along with the change to the modern name, when it was mentioned in the *Paston Letters*, that fascinating annal of a local family's struggle to survive in very testing times. In one of those domestic sidelights that make the *Paston Letters* so human, John writes to Margaret of a visitor: "I pray you make him of good cheer, and if it be so that he tarry, I must remember his costs; therefore if I shall be sent for, and he tarry at Norwich the while, it were best to set his horse at the Maydes Hedde, and I shall be content for the expenses."

There is a Tudor inglenook and hearth, and Elizabeth I stayed here on one of her countless progresses. There is also a curiosity: a Jacobean oak booth, which is always described as a bar, although bars as we know them post-date James I by some 200 years. Whatever the origins of this oddity, it was imported into an inn, which was developing both as a local social centre and as a nodal point for travellers. As well as a coaching inn – the Norwich Machine went to the Green Dragon, Bishopsgate, three times a week, taking a day, in the early days of the coach trade – the

Maids Head was a venue for city social gatherings including balls, exhibitions, and concerts. The local freemasons' lodge was formed here.

In modern times, the Maids Head was rescued by a local historian, Walter Rye, a member of that fraternity of idealists which included John Fothergill to whom innkeeping had a more than purely commercial significance. Thomas Burke recorded, in 1930, that Rye took over the inn not through personal ambition but because the owner of many years was about to sell it and Rye feared that a big brewer would buy it, and that "it would be turned into a commercial inn, with a coloured glass bar, a billiard-room, and the rest of it; and, in fact, that the whole place was to be spoiled and no longer be a refuge for those who like peace and quiet and old surroundings."

Rye's indulgence – he stuffed his inn with antiques and installed luxuries such as electricity and hot water – cost him thousands, but he set standards for which we should still thank him today.

Above Some Tudor framework survives alongside the neo-classical front.

SCOLE INN
SCOLE

The Scole Inn, once the White Hart, is unusual in being more famous for what isn't there than for what is. Not that there's anything wrong with what is there, which is a purpose-built 17th-century inn, created for the richest class of business traveller. But one can't help missing what is no longer there.

The inn was built in 1655, by a Norwich merchant, James Peck, at the junction of two key routes, one linking Norwich and Ipswich, and the other linking Lowestoft to Thetford, Cambridge, and the Midlands. It was built in the finest style. Its mellow red brick is a rarity for the area and had to be imported from the Midlands at great expense. The stylish design incorporates tall moulded brick chimneys and elaborate Dutch gables, which would have made merchants visiting from the Low Countries feel very much at home.

Its original fittings were splendid: they included a round bed, which allegedly could accommodate 20 not-too-fussy couples, more than double the capacity of the much better-known Great Bed of Ware.

Above The entire building dates from the mid-17th century.

The inn's lost glory was its sign. Carved by a man named Fairchild, the sign spanned the road and was loaded with mythical figures, depicting the legend of *Diana and Actaeon*. Actaeon, you recall, was turned into a white hart by Diana because he accidentally saw the Chaste Goddess bathing naked in a rock-pool. Surely, if she was so touchy about being spotted in her nothings, she could either have bathed in private or kept her cossie on? Actaeon, however, never got the chance to point out how unreasonable she was being, as he was promptly ripped apart by his own hounds.

Fairchild's sign was a marvel in its day, with 25 classical figures on the crossbeam and Hades with Cerberus and Charon at the feet of the uprights. It also carried the armorial bearings of Peck, his wife, and

12 other leading local families. It cost the staggering sum of £1,057 and was a popular subject for artists. Sadly, all we are left with are their engravings, since the sign was allowed to rot and vanished in about 1800.

The White Hart barely survived the loss of its coach trade to the London-Norwich railway line, which passed through neighbouring Diss, Much of the complex was let to various tenants for most of the 19th century and, as late as the 1920s, Charles Harper could only describe it as "once magnificent". You will be delighted to hear that it has now been restored to the condition its founder intended.

Above The red-brick theme is continued inside.

NORTHAMPTONSHIRE

TALBOT
OUNDLE

The title of the Oldest Inn in England is a hotly-disputed one, made no easier to settle by the fact that there are different ways of judging it.

Is the Oldest Inn in England the same as the oldest building in use as an inn? If so, then the Fighting Cocks at St Albans, a medieval dovecote, is a strong contender. Or is the Oldest Inn in England the same as the building in longest continuous use as an inn? That knocks out the Fighting Cocks, a comparative stripling of three or four centuries. It is also, I'm glad to say, quite impossible to judge, as the nature of the evidence is so contradictory and fragmentary. Why glad? Because, if it were ever finally resolved, scores of licensees, if not hundreds, would instantly be deprived of their proudest boast.

The Talbot bases its claim to seniority on yet a third measure of antiquity, which is to award the title to the site in longest continuous use as an inn, irrespective of the age of the actual building. This is like asking whether an axe whose head and handle have both been replaced is the same axe or not. Anyway, the Talbot claims to date from 638, when a monastic guest-house was founded on the site, the monastery itself standing on the site now occupied by Oundle School.

It remained in ecclesiastical hands even after the dissolution, when it came into the possession of the Guild of Our Lady of Oundle and was known as the Tabard. A guest one night, in February 1587, was the headsman, on his way to Fotheringhay Castle a few miles off where, the next day, he relieved Mary Queen of Scots of her bonce.

By a neat twist of irony, the inn's owner in 1626, William Whitwell, used stone rescued from the Castle, then in the process of demolition, to build a new three-gabled front for the Talbot, as he renamed it.

Overleaf The stone used to re-front the Talbot came from Fotheringhay Castle.

A few years later, he also bought the Castle's staircase, complete with its oddly-shaped transom window, which is still glazed with horn, not glass. The ghost on the stair is said to be that of Mary herself, descending for the last time from the apartment where she had been confined. The presence in the courtyard, however, is more of a portent than a ghost, and takes the form of a slow drumbeat coming from an old well, long filled in. It manifests itself, as these phenomena do, in times of England's greatest need and gives its name to nearby Drummingwell Lane.

Above The staircase and window were once part of Fotheringhay Castle.

SARACENS HEAD
TOWCESTER

D o not be fooled by the rather stern demeanour of the Saracens Head. It's purely an illusion created by the dour brown Barnack stone used on the frontage and, inside, all is as cheery and welcoming as it was when Sam Weller urged Mr Pickwick who, with his companions, had driven up from Coventry in pouring rain, to lodge here with the following recommendation:

"There's beds here. Everything's clean and very comfortable. Wery good little dinner, sir, they can get ready in half an hour – pair o' fowls, sir, and a weal cutlet; french beans, taturs, tarts, and tidiness. You'd better stop where you are sir, if I might recommend."

At this point, the landlord appeared "to confirm Mr Weller's statement relative to the accommodations of the establishment and to back his entreaties with a variety of dismal conjectures regarding the state of the roads, the doubt of fresh horses being to be had at the next stage, the dead certainty of its raining all night, and other topics of inducement familiar to innkeepers." The room to which the Pickwickians were shown was called the Sun, where a cheerful fire was laid and the table was lit with wax candles. "Everything looked (as everything always does in all decent English inns) as if the travellers had been expected, and their comforts prepared for days beforehand."

Here, Mr Pickwick and his companions encountered the pompous rival newspaper editors, Pott of the Eatanswill Gazette and Slurk of the Eatanswill Independent, to start a slanging-match, which concluded late at night in the inn kitchen, "unmitigated viper" and "ungrammatical twaddler" being among the taunts exchanged. One can't help wondering if they were portraits of editors Dickens himself knew.

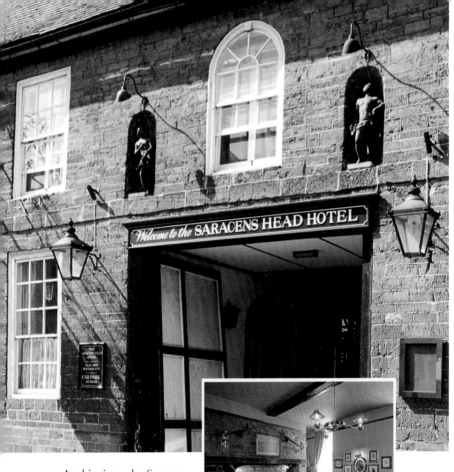

At this time, the Saracens Head was about 150 years old and was one of many coaching inns in this strategically-sited town, which stands at the junction of the Watling Street and the main Oxford-Northampton road. It changed its name to the Pomfret Arms in 1831, to attract the patronage of the Earls of Pomfret, who lived nearby until the family died out in 1867. Dickens preferred to use the original name, to which the inn has recently returned.

Above and Inset The inn's cosy interior compensates for the rather foreboding exterior.

NORTHUMBERLAND

ANGEL
CORBRIDGE

It's hard to forget the Romans so close to Hadrian's Wall. Roads here are ramrod straight; Roman masonry peers at you from the walls of field, barn, and cottage; and every town and village, it seems, has the rubble of a Roman fort or vicus between its toes.

Nowhere is this more evident than in Corbridge, *Corstopitum* to the auxiliary units that manned the Wall for most of its nearly 300 years of active service. The town lay not actually on the Wall, but a few miles south. It was the depot where all the army's needs – grain, remounts, leather, iron, wine, and all the countless minutiae necessary to sustain a military society – were exchanged. The civilians here must have been rich, for rivers of gold raised by the harsh taxation of the more peaceful provinces of the Empire ran through their fingers.

The Angel is not quite as old as the Wall, although it does possess, in a glass case on a window ledge in the saloon, a very worn and weathered carved stone head, possibly Roman, possibly British – for the Celts had a cult of the severed head and, when Romanised, took to adorning wells and springs with carvings of them. A sacred legend, albeit diminished by the passage of centuries, attaches to the Angel's graven head: a horrid fate – a car crash, not winning the lottery – befalls anyone who moves it.

If it is not quite Roman, the Angel is certainly medieval and may have been a hospice of the Abbey of Hexham, three miles away. If it was the monks' inn, the irony will not have been lost on the commissioners who, in 1539, chose it as their lodging while supervising the Abbey's surrender.

The Angel survived the dissolution as a well-appointed and, standing as it did at the junction of the Edinburgh-London and Carlisle-Newcastle routes, a well-sited inn. In due course, it became the town's

principal coaching inn and, in the unusually broad street outside, then an open space, local people would gather to hear the landlord read the latest news, freshly delivered by the London mail.

A visit in the 1950s inspired Denzil Batchelor to rhapsodise about the Northumbrian cuisine, which, even in his day, was dying out. Local salmon was then a great delicacy, with the poorer cuts being pickled like gravadlax – an echo of the region's Norse heritage? Pickled salmon might be served reheated with pan haggerty, a griddle-cake of cheese and onion, layered between thinly-sliced potato. Other specialities havered between sweet and savoury: Felton spiced loaf, with almonds and lemon, is now a teacake but, like mince pies, was probably once a heavily-spiced savoury; while singin' hinnies are griddle cakes that contain currants, but are traditionally cooked with mutton fat.

The Angel today, refaced like so many coaching inns in Georgian times, is a handsome, comfortable hotel, with an elegantly-panelled lounge. Sadly, it is no longer known for its traditional local dishes.

Above An original 16th-century door survives amidst the Georgian renovations.

NOTTINGHAMSHIRE

YE OLDE BELL

BARNBY MOOR

Ye Olde Bell tells a common story: that of the great coaching inn which closed its doors when rail swept the roads of traffic, only to open them again when cars succeeded coaches.

The inn dates from the 16th century, and was a farm fronting the Great North Road some distance from the village of Barnby Moor itself, until passing coaches created a business opportunity more profitable

Above The inn still retains an air of the farmhouse it originally was.

than agriculture. Its site, in the middle of a long and bleak stretch of the road, made the Bell a particularly welcome stop for weary travellers, such as Thomas Twyning who, in 1776, referred to it as "a gentleman-like, comfortable house".

Soon after 1784, when mail coaches began to replace the mounted post-boys who had previously carried the mail, the Blue Bell, as it was by now known, became a stage for the London-Edinburgh mail. It was a substantial enough inn for Princess Victoria to stay in on her way to York in 1835. The owner then was George Clarke, a celebrity in the racing world, who stabled 120 horses at the Blue Bell and at the White Horse in the village itself. His death from gout in 1842, after 42 years at the inn, coincided very nearly with the end of coaching. The London-Edinburgh mail stopped in 1845 and, with it, went the Blue Bell's entire livelihood, for it was too far from the village even to survive as a pub.

Instead, it was sold as a private house to a Mr Beever and, in the next 60 years, the old pond, whose purpose had been the tightening of carriage wheels, was filled in; the stables became cottages, except for a small area, which was converted into a chapel; and the house itself was divided into two parts.

Then came cars, and with them the revival of the Great North Road. A speculator restored the property as an inn in 1904 – the aisle of the chapel is now the corridor between rooms 5 and 17 – but failed twice to get a licence, partly due to objections from the licensee of the White Horse. In 1906, though, the support of the Road Club of Great Britain persuaded the justices to change their minds, and the inn was reborn (now with the "Ye Olde" tag).

There was another brief period of closure during World War One but, otherwise, the inn flourished until 1953, when two wings were completely destroyed by fire one night when the hotel was packed with racegoers attending the St Leger at Doncaster. It was then rebuilt incorporating antique panelling from two local great houses, Wiseton Hall and Bradgate House which, like so many other hard-to-maintain country houses at the time, were being demolished.

SARACENS HEAD
SOUTHWELL

Southwell's splendid Norman minster was founded in 1110, but the Saracens Head predates it, for fragments of the timber frame have been tentatively dated as 11th century. It was definitely the Kings Arms as early as 1194, when it was visited by Richard I. He was the first of a long list of royal guests, attesting to the inn's strategic location on the Great North Road. John stayed in 1213; as did Henry III in 1223 and 1258; Edward I in 1281; Edward III in 1331; and Richard II in 1395, 1396, and 1398.

The inn was the property of the Archdiocese of York – one reason, perhaps, for its succession of royal visitors – and was leased in 1396 to a John Fisher, who set about rebuilding it. Its prominence continued undimmed. Edward IV stayed in 1481 and Cardinal Wolsey, after his disgrace, in 1530. James I passed through on his way to claim his throne in 1603, declaring the town's minster to be the equal of Durham or York, "or any other kirk in Christendom".

Charles I stayed here in August 1642, after raising his standard at Nottingham, too afraid of the mob to stay in the city itself. He spent his last night of freedom here, on 5 May 1646, with his chaplain Dr Hudson and a follower called Ashburnham. Charles himself posed as Ashburnham's servant, probably not very

Left The sash windows were added in 1805.

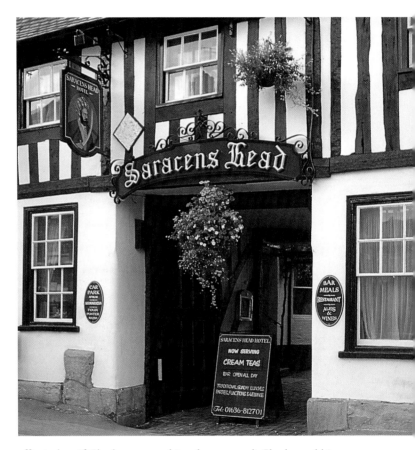

effectively – if Charles was anything, he was regal! Charles and his party met the French ambassador to Scotland, Montreuil, and hosted the Scottish commissioners, who were staying at the Bishop's palace, for dinner. The next day, in the inn's coffee-room, Charles surrendered to the Scots, who sold him to Cromwell for £400,000. He was beheaded – the last English king to die a violent death – in January 1649.

Above The old carriage arch now serves as the inn's main entrance.

The bedroom, in which the Church of England's only saint spent his last night of freedom is still pointed out to visitors to the Saracens Head. In 1858, the awestruck Bishop of New Zealand, Dr Selwyn, tried and failed to sleep in it and sat up writing a long, sentimental, repetitive set of couplets, of which none, alas, are quite bad enough to quote. The inn's name was changed in 1652, after Charles II's ill-fated Worcester campaign. The new name was a secret royalist sign, since the young Charles was famously swarthy as a result of his Medici ancestry.

Later, the Saracens Head became a profitable posting house between Nottingham and the Great North Road at Newark. It was also, for a time, the local Inland Revenue office. In 1805, it was plastered over, sashes were inserted, and the town Assembly Room next door was incorporated. Byron, the greatest romantic poet of them all and a local resident, knew the place well and, in 1807, wrote an epitaph for a local carrier and drunk which, as with Selwyn, is too long but, in this case, not quite good enough to quote.

About a century later, Harper wrote: "Southwell has fallen into a dreamless slumber since the last of the coaches left and, as the traveller comes into its quiet streets he feels that he has come into a place whose days of activity ended considerably over half a century ago." The Saracens Head, however, has come through the test of centuries pretty well so far. Nothing seems likely to stand between it and a few more centuries of the same.

OXFORDSHIRE

RED LION
ADDERBURY

The Red Lion is one of those pubs that is not particularly grand, nor particularly ancient, nor particularly historic, but which embodies all the qualities required of the traditional English inn. Good food, and good beer are all there, housed in a picturesque old stone building.

The Red Lion's Tudor roots were uncovered during restoration work, when two coats of arms – of Henry VIII and the local Bustard family – were found under a layer of plaster in a bedroom. At the same time, lath-and-plaster infill was discovered, suggesting an early date.

With Banbury so near by, the Red Lion was hardly in the ideal location to succeed as a coaching inn, but the level of comfort provided there – witness the elegant drawing-room with its fine fireplaces, and other 17th-century fireplaces to be found in the bedrooms – proved attractive to the better sort of traveller. Indeed, the Red Lion was known for a time as the Travellers' Inn.

Adderbury, so peaceful now, suffered badly in the Civil War, when the Roundheads constantly sought to outflank the Royal

Above Age-blackened beams, wooden panelling, and cheery fires are found inside.

capital, Oxford, and cut it off from its hinterland to the West. Adderbury was the scene of many skirmishes, and the secret tunnel of legend is supposed to have formed an escape route for Royalists. This supposes that the Royalists expected defeat far enough in advance to start work on a secret tunnel. Where they planned to escape to is not clear, since the tunnel never got much further than its beginnings in the inn cellar.

The landlord in 1669, Thomas Austin, was respectable and reliable enough to mint his own trade tokens. His son, Thomas jnr, was neither: he was arrested in 1687 for refusing to support his illegitimate child.

The well in the yard is believed to have provided water for a brewhouse in what is now the dining-room. Brewing would have stopped in the 1950s, when Hall's of Oxford bought the Red Lion from the Townsend family, who had owned it for over a century. The inn is now part of the Old English chain.

Overleaf The Red Lion overlooks Adderbury's village green.

Above and Right The Old Bull is the only building in the street with a brick front.

OLD BULL
BURFORD

In a famous Cotswold high street – perhaps the most famous of all Cotswold high streets – the Old Bull at Burford stands out from the other buildings.

Stone – gloriously mellow, deep tawny-golden stone – is one the distinguishing marks of the region. High windswept plateaux and narrow wooded combes you can find anywhere. Rambling old farms, soaring church towers, haughty Georgian mansions – these are not unique. No, the spell of the Cotswolds lies in its stone, that most magical, most malleable, most beautiful of all building materials. But you can have too much of a good thing and, whoever decided to clad the Old Bull in distinguishing brick, made a commercially wise choice.

The original Bull, owned by a family of distinguished vintners named Hannes, was three doors down. When they sold up, in 1607, their tenant, John Silvester, moved to the present site and set up again under the same name. The house, which he leased from the parish, is known from the mid-15th century, and a cottage on the site, which also belongs to the Bull, has some early 14th-century work. Over the course of a generation, Silvester and his heirs converted this jumble of medieval tenements into a single inn – complete with brick front.

The work was doubtless hindered by the Civil War, which, on one occasion, saw Prince Rupert and 1,000 cavalry descend on the town seeking donations. On New Year's Eve 1642, Royalist troops quartered in the Bull were attacked by Roundhead dragoons. In 1649, a mutiny by 900 Levellers was crushed in the town by Cromwell in person: 350 of them were locked up in the church and the leaders were summarily shot.

After the war, Burford boomed as a resort. It had a fashionable race-course; entertainments such as the annual Vension Feast drew pleasure-seekers from a wide area; and diversions available at its inns throughout the 18th century included "card and dance" assemblies and travelling players. The Bull, with its splendid Market Room, was the scene of many of these entertainments, staging plays and hosting the ball that followed the Venison Feast. It also had a well used cockpit.

Burford stands at the junction of five coach routes and, as coach travel increased, the Bull's business grew. It grew physically, too, absorbing the little Talbot Inn next to its yard on Witney Street in 1707. The last coach passed through in 1850, and no railway came to replace it. Choked of custom, the annual races ended. The Venison Feast was suspended.In the agricultural depression, which started in the 1870s, even the weekly market failed. The Bull survived as a commercial hotel. Burford was rediscovered in the motoring age and, once again, became a tourist trap.

Today, the Old Bull is all ancient beams and Jacobean panelling, with a closed-in gallery. It drips antiquity – but it is all reconditioned. The inn was badly damaged by fire in 1982. The entire front had to be taken down and reassembled. The internal fittings, charred, smoke-blackened, and waterlogged, had to be sieved out of the wreckage, and either restored or replaced. They didn't do a bad job, did they?

GEORGE

DORCHESTER-ON-THAMES

The story of Dorchester's venerable inn is intimately linked with the story of the equally venerable abbey church, just across the road, founded in 635 by the Roman missionary St Birinus, who converted the local king.

Above The George has retained its galleried front.

The church at Dorchester was a cathedral until 1070, when the see was transferred to Lincoln. Only three buildings survived the Dissolution: the church itself, now the parish church; the abbot's guest-house, now the museum; and the common hospitium, built in 1450, now the George Inn.

The abbey and its estate were purchased by a Richard Bewfforest in 1540. He donated the church to the parish and kept the guest-house as an inn. It prospered from the start, as it was well-placed for travellers at the crossing of the River Thame. In the Civil War, the town was a vital frontier position for the King's capital at Oxford, and had a garrison of 1,000, whose victualling needs can have done the George's trade no harm at all.

After the war, the George became a major coach-stop, a status it held for 150 years. But part of the building had to be sold off as a private house in 1840, and a wheelwright rented the yard. For a long time, the old George was not much more than a small-town pub, albeit a cheery one. The cricket writer Denzil Batchelor knew it well in the 1950s and '60s, when it was run by a man named Joe Jordan, who was 20 stone, and his wife, who was 18 stone. "They slept in the same bed," marvelled Batchelor, who also praised the inn for its hospitality. It's rather grander than that today, but not so grand as to be anything less than welcoming.

RED LION

HENLEY

This Georgian hotel, on its 15th-century foundations, has been entertaining the rich and famous, among them Charles I, almost from its very beginning.

The Red Lion's fortune has always been its setting at one end of the bridge carrying the London road over the Thames. In coaching days, as its *porte-cochère* testifies, the inn was used both by public carriages and by the more lucrative private post-chaises. Once coaching was done, the

Above The Red Lion is built from mellow red brick.

long riverside range became the more valuable part of the property. Its private rooms afforded the opportunity to watch the Regatta as it should be watched – in the utmost luxury. In fact, the Red Lion is luxurious throughout: its so-called snug bar is more like a Pall Mall club than any snug bar I've ever drunk light and bitter in.

The Red Lion is also part of a triangular literary argument. It always used to be said that the poet Shenstone first scratched the famous last verse of "Lines Written At An Inn" (you know it: "Whoe'er has travelled life's dull round, Where'er his stages may have been, May sigh to think how oft he found, The warmest welcome – at an Inn.") on a window pane here, and that the preceding stanzas were written later.

This may not seem much of a controversy to you and me in our busy lives but, in a more leisured age, it really mattered that the honour was also claimed for the White Swan at Henley-in-Arden, Shenstone's home town, and the long-vanished Sunrising Inn on Edge Hill, near Banbury.

One suspects that the people to whom it mattered most were the proprietors of the three inns, since the poem, also known as "Freedom", is one of the best advertisements for the virtues of the inn ever penned. Whoever could say that it had been inspired by his own house had the best testimonial of all time. It was also an argument that enthused literary critics for generations.

According to Shenstone's biographer Richard Graves, the poem was actually written in the arbour at the Sunrising Inn in 1750. But the stanza was quite plainly scratched on a window at the Red Lion too, and it was argued that Shenstone, who often travelled between Henley-in-Arden and London on the coach that called at the Red Lion, may have scratched it here as well. He was, after all, very proud of his best-known work. Anyway, as Harper observed in recounting the story: "There is no disabling the flying canard."

SHAVEN CROWN

SHIPTON-UNDER-WYCHWOOD

I s the Shaven Crown the most beautiful pub in the country? I ask this
question in all seriousness. Of course, it can't be answered; but then
if it were, books like this would never be written. Anyway, my
tentative, but not entirely arbitrary, answer is: yes. It's based on applying
the following scale.

Imagine you have eaten lunch in the bar. You're now passing
the afternoon sitting outside with another pint. How do you feel?
If diesel-smuts from the lorries thundering past are turning the

Above The old carriage arch now serves as an entrance hall.

artificially-gassed head on your pint of keg beer a nasty grey; if the scenery is all concrete, tarmac, and piles of empty beer barrels; if the overpriced food, prepared in a distant factory and reheated, has left a nasty slick of fat on your tongue, then you're in the car park of a Beefeater on the A45 in Birmingham. Score: zero.

If, on the other hand, you're in a fragrant garden in a 14th-century Cotswold stone courtyard; if the food was great and the beer is better; if everything is beautiful and nothing hurts, you're at the Shaven Crown at Shipton-under-Wychwood. Score: 10. (Add a bonus point if someone else is driving.)

The Shaven Crown is the sort of place that doesn't really need a biography: seeing and feeling is enough. But, for the record, it was built in about 1330, as a guest-house for Bruerne Priory, and became a royal hunting lodge after the Dissolution. Queen Elizabeth I presented it to the village, to be rented out to pay for poor relief; the village sold it only in 1922, reinvesting the proceeds as a charitable trust.

To this day, the inn retains its great hall, open to the roof, as well as its cobbled carriage-arch, now the entrance hall where the original double doors are still displayed. Only two things have changed since Charles Harper visited it at about the time of its sale. He noted that all the original mullions, except the one next to the arch, had been replaced by sashes: today, they are mullions again. And, in his day, it was called just the plain old Crown. The Shaven bit is evidently a rather feeble pun on the inn's monastic origins. It's the only flaw in an otherwise perfect pub.

Above Original beams can be seen in the roof of the great hall.

SPREADEAGLE
THAME

The breadth of Thame's high street, and the Georgian severity of the Spreadeagle's long frontage – constructed of a hard salt-glazed brick so unweathered that it could almost be 1930s Post Office neo-classical – speak of a substantial coach and posting trade in years gone by. As does the elaborate inn sign, made by a blacksmith from neighbouring Long Crendon in the 1820s.

But the Spreadeagle's claim to posterity has nothing to do with its more distant past and everything to do with John Fothergill, the Pioneer Amateur Innkeeper, whom we met at the Three Swans in Market Harborough, Leicestershire.

One of the best accounts of Fothergill is given by the man himself, in *An Innkeeper's Diary* and *My Three Inns*. He came to innkeeping needing a trade and made an art of it, but – as so often happens with artists – made no money. Since his first two or three years at the Spreadeagle were spent alienating every regular customer it had, that may not come as a surprise. But, as he makes clear, it was scarcely rubbing along even when he arrived, so perhaps his efforts to reposition it (to use marketing jargon) were not as unreasonable as his own writings sometimes make them seem. It's interesting to read between the lines of his work, to see how such an inn had survived the

Above The elaborate cast-iron sign hints at the inn's past prosperity.

Above The old coach arch was still a feature in the Geogian renovations.

collapse of coaching. There were the farmers on market day, whose 2/6 lunch, Fothergill reckoned, cost him 4/6; there were charabanc trips from the poorer parts of London, and motoring club days out from the better-off; there were commercial travellers; there was the hunt; there were race meetings; there were the Freemasons; and there was the annual agricultural show. The old coach-house was also let out as storage to a market trader, although Fothergill sent him packing before enquiring how much rent, if any, he paid.

All these sources of revenue Fothergill drove away, seeking to replace them with custom from Oxford dons and undergraduates, society friends of his, and smart visitors, such as the Spanish royal party, who turned up unannounced and ate nothing.

"I've determined not only to have proper and properly cooked food, but to have only either intelligent, beautiful, or well-bred people to eat it," he declared at the outset. And, when things went wrong, he explained: "When we came here, we had to stand and wait for our custom. We depended upon the visitations of the farmers, the Freemasons, the Grammar School dinner, race meetings, rent audits, people held up by fog. I can't describe what an anxiety this was."

The Spreadeagle may have been a commercial flop, but it was a *succès d'estime*. Thomas Burke – who could be no less precious than Fothergill – wrote of it: "If one sees the inn generally as a sound and sensible institution, then among inns the Spreadeagle is witty. It is witty in its spirit, in its decorations, and particularly in its meals. We all know the regular inn lunch, but whatever you get at the Spreadeagle you won't get that. I can't describe the dishes I have eaten there; I can't even name their constituents; I can only say that they were new to me and that I would like to eat them again."

Fothergill sold up to a London businessman who owned a chain of butcher's shops and, when he moved, his spirit moved with him. Today, the Spreadeagle is a soundly-run but unexceptional hotel, where Fothergill's idiosyncrasies are remembered, but where, sensibly, no attempt is made to perpetuate them.

BEAR
WOODSTOCK

Woodstock is one of those places which, to the foreign observer, is a perfect metaphor for England. Here, the elegant town-houses of the gentry rub shoulders with the humble yet quaint cottages of respectful peasants. Dominating all, aloof yet all-pervading, is Blenheim Palace in its walled park.

The park in which the palace stands, and the money to pay for its building, were voted to John Churchill, Duke of Marlborough, by a grateful and very relieved nation for his outstanding generalship in a long and ultimately triumphant war against overwhelming odds. People forget it now, but Queen Anne's England feared invasion just as much as George III's or George VI's. Vanburgh built the palace; the wall around its park is seven miles long.

In giving Woodstock to Churchill, Queen Anne was giving away property that had been in the royal domain for at least 700 years. Ethelred the Unready held the manor in person; to his heirs it was a much-loved royal hunting ground. Henry II did more than hunt deer here: it was where he kept his mistress, Rosamund Clifford, Fair Rosamund of the ballad. Two centuries later, the Black Prince was born here; and, during the brief reign of Bloody Mary, Princess Elizabeth was imprisoned here.

Such an important place needed inns to lodge those who came to petition the King – for, in the Middle Ages, where the King was, there the Capital was. Indeed, in grants of land in Woodstock made by Henry II to his followers, the building of hostelries is specifically purposed.

The Bear claims to have been one of these hostelries, although you'd never guess it. But scratch the surface and you'll find the inn's true age. There are 13th-century cobbles beneath the red carpet in reception, once the carriage arch; and oak beams in the bar are of the same age. Certainly, it fulfils Henry II's expectations: the rich and famous have often chosen it above Woodstock's other inns.

The Bear is haunted: a night porter working in the restaurant looked up to find himself briefly transported back in time, surrounded by benches and trestles, with rushes underfoot and, looming over him, a knight in armour, clearly awaiting the return of the sword, which the porter was busy polishing. Furniture moves. Lights are switched on and off by no human hand. And in one of the bedrooms – I won't tell you which – you are likely to feel and maybe even see and hear the ghost of the chambermaid who hanged herself in it 170 years ago.

Above The Georgian front, with its sash windows, has a rather severe appearance.

RUTLAND

MARQUESS OF EXETER
LYDDINGTON

Rutland, and the adjoining corner of Leicestershire, are relatively undiscovered by tourists; which is strange for, in its own way, the region is as delightful as the Cotswolds. The hills are a little rounder, the uplands a little less bleak. The towns – Uppingham, Oakham, Melton Mowbray – are less assiduously preserved than Burford, Broadway, or Stow-on-the-Wold, but the architecture is just as fine; and the villages are, if anything, even prettier.

The inns are good, too. I could rattle off a long list of them, every one of which you would be a fool not to visit – so I shall: the Exeter Arms, Barrowden; the Fox & Hounds, Exton; the Stag & Hounds, Burrow-on-the-Hill; the Old Brewery Inn, Somerby; the Bell, Frisby-on-the-Wreake; the White Horse, Empingham ... there are so many.

Lyddington, just south of Uppingham, has two such pubs, one at each end, both 17th century in origin, both picturesque, both eminently visitable for their food, beer, and welcome. One is the Old White Horse, and the other is the Marquess of Exeter.

The Marquess of Exeter, like many other inns in the district, is named after Thomas Cecil, eldest son of Elizabeth I's Chancellor, Lord Burghley. A sottish ne'er-do-well in his youth, Thomas was made MP for Stamford in 1563 at the age of 21 and grew into a warrior who revelled in tournaments and fought against the Scots and the Spanish, taking

part in the defeat of the Armada in 1588. Appointed Lord Protector of the North in 1599, he embarked on a fanatical persecution of Roman Catholics, filling his study with the copes and missals of priests he had hanged. In 1601, he put down the Earl of Essex's rebellion and was made Earl of Exeter as a reward. He had 13 children by his first wife and, in 1609, married a woman 38 years younger than himself. He died in 1623 aged 81.

Such bloodthirstiness and lust is a world away from the Marquess of Exeter in Lyddington, a peaceful old place and a good representative of the region's village inns. The oak beams, the low ceilings, the great inglenook, all make the perfect setting for great food, beautifully-kept beers, and a wine-list that is a cut above the average.

Above The whole inn had to be reconstructed after a devastating fire in 1995.

Above Despite its stately appearance, the Georgian inn was built as a coaching house.

SHROPSHIRE

MYTTON & MERMAID
ATCHAM

Two miles east of Shrewsbury, where the Watling Street crosses the Severn near Roman *Viroconium*, is Atcham with its red-brick Georgian coaching inn, the Mytton & Mermaid. It is surrounded by trees, with the volcanic mass of the Wrekin and the village church behind it, the gardens sloping down to the river, and the elegant 18th-century bridge before it. Pevsner described it as stately; so stately, in fact, that it looks more like a country mansion than a pub.

But it really was purpose-built as an inn, to serve the coaching trade that grew up when the main road for Holyhead and Ireland was switched south, from the old northern route through Chester and along the coast, to the new southern one through Shrewsbury and Snowdonia. Originally called the Talbot in honour of the Earls of Shrewsbury, it later changed its name to the Berwick Arms after the Hill family of nearby Attingham Park, who bore the title Lord Berwick.

Steam killed the Berwick Arms within 50 years of its construction. It was a private house for nearly a century after that until, in the 1930s, it was bought by the architect of Portmeirion, Sir Clough Williams-Ellis, who reopened it as the Mytton & Mermaid. The Mermaid component of the name comes from his own coat of arms; Mytton commemorates the squire of Halston, Mad Jack Mytton, MP for Shrewsbury in the mid-18th century, madcap horseman and legendary drinker, immortalised by CJ Apperley (Nimrod) in his *Life Of John Mytton*.

Mytton once rode a bear into a dinner-party; and he went hunting with six broken ribs the day after a fall: it took three bottles of port to see him safely to the finish. Mytton's connection with Atcham, however, is slight: he died demented in debtors' prison at the age of 38, and his body rested a night here on its journey home.

FEATHERS
LUDLOW

If there were a league table of visually exciting inns, indeed of visually exciting buildings, the Feathers would surely be near the top. Even though the frame is an essentially square structure, there is not a single right angle to be seen.

In 1475, Ludlow Castle became the seat of the Council of the Marches and the effective capital of a politically highly-sensitive region. It was from Ludlow Castle that the young Edward V and his younger brother departed in spring 1483 for London and Edward's coronation. Along the way, they fell in with their wicked uncle Richard and, although no one can say exactly what befell them, the one thing we do know is that it was Richard who was crowned, not Edward.

The great families of the March all kept townhouses in Ludlow, and there were many inns for petitioners and other visitors. The original Feathers dates back to this heyday, but only the heavily-studded front door remains of the inn recorded in 1521. The present building, dated 1603, was built as the townhouse of a family called Foxe during the last great flowering of half-timbering. It was eventually bought by a Rees Jones, who turned it into a grand inn. It was named in 1616, to commemorate a visit by the Prince of Wales. The decoration of the first-floor lounge includes an oak overmantel, a cast iron fireback, and a moulded plaster ceiling, all carrying the royal coat of arms.

The Council of the Marches was wound up in 1689, and the town fell on hard times. The Feathers closed until 1752, when a Samuel Corne reopened it as a posting-house with stabling for 60 horses. It shared trade with the nearby Bull and the classical Angel, now closed, in Broad Street.

Even after the collapse of coaching, it carried on as a hotel both for commercials and tourists for, even when Ludlow lost its regional status, it remained both the economic hub of a large farming area and – for reasons you will appreciate if you are lucky enough to visit – a magnet for visitors.

Previous page Every timber in the Feathers' front is elaborately carved in gothic style.

LION
SHREWSBURY

You would not think it now but, less than a century ago, this greatest of historic inns was, commercially, on its knees: a semi-derelict, redundant old pile, plainly about to cash in its chips. It would have been a dreadful shame if, at that nadir, its fortunes had sunk just below the level at which it would have been more profitable to close it, tear it down, and build some dreadful red-brick draper's or dairy or "chambers" on the site. For the Lion has old bones and stories to tell.

By repute, Henry IV stayed here on the eve of the Battle of Shrewsbury in 1402, and young Henry Tudor rested here in 1485 on his triumphant journey from exile to Bosworth and foundation of a dynasty. Certainly, ancient remnants have been excavated in its fabric, but the first reliable record of an inn on the site is not until 1618, and the Lion's first days of greatness belong to the turn of the 18th and 19th centuries, and a great entrepreneur of the coaching age in particular.

The career of Robert Lawrence and the great days of the Lion are discussed in the introductory chapter. Lawrence died full of honour in 1806, and is buried in the churchyard of St Julian's (a church no longer) beneath an epitaph extolling his "public spirit and unremitting exertions in opening the great road through Wales between the United Kingdoms, as also for establishing the first mail coach to this town". For some years, the Lion continued as before: Dickens visited with his illustrator Hablot Browne in 1838 and found nothing to complain about. They were put up in an annexe and Dickens wrote to his daughter: "We have the strangest little room. The windows bulge out over the street as if they were the stern windows of a ship. A door opens from the sitting-room on to a little open gallery with plants on it, where one leans over a queer old rail." (The stern windows and queer old rail are still to be seen, and leaned over, to this day.)

Above and Right The Lion has now been fully restored.

But Washington Irving, in 1855, found that, although the Lion was still functioning, it had sadly decayed since the railway replaced the coaches. It was, he said, "an uncheerful old hotel which takes it upon itself to be in the best class of English country hotels and charges the best prices; very dark in the lower apartments, and pervaded with a musty odour."

It was still the town's principal inn but, by 1906, Charles Harper found it all but moribund: the "fine broad stone stairway" to the ballroom was "much chipped, dirty, and neglected". Dances were still held there on occasion, but its main use was as a commercial travellers' stockroom. "On the ground floor is the billiard-room of

the present day, formerly the coach dining-room," wrote Harper. "In crepuscular apartments adjoining, in these times given over to forgotten lumber, the curious may find the deserted kitchens of a bygone age, with the lifts and hatches to upper floors that once conveyed their abundant meals to a vanished generation of John Bulls."

Shortly after Harper's visit, the Lion was rescued by Trust Houses.

SOMERSET

LUTTRELL ARMS
DUNSTER

The Luttrell Arms is a truly glorious example of the way vastly different styles and periods of architecture and decor can combine in perfect aesthetic harmony.

Built as a townhouse for the Abbots of Cleeve, three miles away, in about 1450, it was acquired by the Luttrells, lords of the manor since 1376, after the Dissolution and opened as an inn called the Ship (Dunster was at that time a small but busy port). The most impressive survivals of the earliest age of the building are the magnificent hammerbeam roof in the main hall and the huge elaborately-carved gothic rear window, which originally looked out on the harbour.

The next layer of building can be traced to the commission of George Luttrell, who died in 1629. His main legacy is the work of the itinerant Dutch craftsmen, who created the magnificent, if somewhat primitive, plasterwork overmantels that dot the inn. Actaeon and Diana, a common theme of the period, are there, as are two caryatids, the arms of England and France, and a figure variously held to be James I or Luttrell himself. This plasterwork may be unsophisticated – Harper calls it amateurish – but is evidence of the prosperity of the local weaving industry at the time: the covered yarn market dates to 1609.

The Ship endured a brief siege at the end of the first civil war, as Parliamentary forces conducted mopping-up operations in this Royalist district. It escaped unscathed, however, to grow fat on the coach traffic using the main road from Bristol through Somerset and into Devon and Cornwall. On the back of this trade, followed the third major rebuilding in 1779, when the inn was given its present name, the frontage was "classicised", ancient mullioned windows were replaced with sashes, and a large extension was added at the back.

The death of coaching did the Luttrell Arms no harm whatsoever, as mass tourism brought by rail to Minehead followed soon after. The old inn, the picturesque market, and the castle on its eminence rapidly, and deservedly, became a major attraction, iconic of Olde England and cream teas. Don't be fooled by the castle, though: it's a Victorian fake.

Above The inn was originally built as a townhouse.

GEORGE & PILGRIMS
GLASTONBURY

Glastonbury, with its mysterious tor rising steeply out of the flat Isle of Avalon, is the mystical navel of England. Here, ancient Britons lived in stilted houses, crossing the marshes on timber causeways. Here, Joseph of Arimathea brought the boy Jesus and planted his staff, which took root to become the Abbey's strange Christmas-flowering thorn. Here, King Arthur was carried, wounded in

Above The building's front survives from 1475.

his final battle, to hide in the Isle of Glass until Britain's direst need; and here, a real king, Alfred, hid from the Danes, waging guerrilla war, gathering strength, and burning cakes before sallying forth to victory.

It is entirely fitting, therefore, that Glastonbury's principal inn should be one of the country's finest surviving 15th-century townhouses. Built by Abbot Selwood in 1475, to replace an earlier inn on the site, the George was designed to accommodate the wealthier of the pilgrims who flocked to the abbey. The front is as cleverly designed and elaborately executed as that of any church of the period and is, according to Sir Albert Richardson, "one of the finest surviving examples of a contemporary design in panelled stonework, at this period such a distinctive feature of the town buildings of the West Country".

In a narrow street frontage, the designer incorporated strong vertical elements, including tall arched windows, a three-storey bay, narrow statuary niches, and squared columns. To balance this upward emphasis, he introduced horizontal string courses at each floor and an armorial panel over the central squared arch. The result is to foster the impression of soaring height beloved by gothic builders, but to offset it with an illusion of width.

Although the abbey was destroyed in the Dissolution, its guest-house survived as the George Inn. Legend puts Henry VIII at a window, watching the abbey burn and its abbot being dragged off to martyrdom.

The George never became a major coaching inn, which is perhaps why its front has survived – apart from the destruction of its statuary by Puritan iconoclasts. It attracted a lot of local posting trade and the narrow carriage-arch was once the access for post-chaises using the stables, now sadly demolished, in the yard at the back.

Inside the George are many oak beams, a supposedly haunted bedroom known as the Monk's Cell, a stone stillage in the cellar known as the penitent's stool, an original staircase, and a fireplace surrounded by Delft tiles, all of them 18th century except one. Traditionally, guests are invited to spot the exception, which is blindingly obvious once it has been pointed out to you.

TALBOT

MELLS

Little Jack Horner sat in a corner, eating his Christmas pie. He put in his thumb and pulled out a plum and said: "What a good boy am I."

A nonsense rhyme? Maybe. But there have been plenty of mythographers prepared to believe it, and a story has even been concocted to explain the rhyme. John Horner, goes the story, was steward to the last Abbot of Glastonbury, who was entrusted by his master to convey the deeds of 12 of the abbey's manors to Henry VIII, in a desperate effort to buy him off during the Dissolution of the monasteries. The documents were concealed in a pie, in case Horner was robbed on the way. But he, knowing the attempt was doomed, took the opportunity to remove one of the deeds – the deeds to the manor of Mells, as it happens – to keep for his own.

The manor – and the lovely old stone-built Talbot – still belong to Horner's descendants, which seems to add credibility. But, as the current lord of the manor, the Earl of Oxford & Asquith, points out, his ancestor Thomas (not John) Horner bought the manor fair and square from the Crown for £1,832 in 1543, five years after Glastonbury was suppressed.

The rhyme is unfair to Richard Whiting, the last Abbot, too. In fact, he was one of the few who refused to surrender to Henry. He endured months of imprisonment and torment while efforts were made to get him to surrender the Abbey and its lands and, when he refused, he was charged with robbery (a charge of treason was dropped as tending to make a martyr) and executed.

The pages of history, even of a gentle domestic history such as this, are splashed with the blood of brave men. Indeed, the connection that the old stones have with the tumults of the past adds, I find, a charge to the experience of drinking and dining there. In the case of the 15th-century Talbot, the old inn yard is the place to relax if the weather permits.

Mells is rather off the beaten track, and because of the lack of passing traffic, the Talbot was, inevitably, used more as a local posting-house and livery than a coaching inn proper. Its little rustic yard has never been spoilt and is now a delightful garden. The interior also retains the multiplicity of snugs and parlours, which is the traditional design, and in my view preferable alternative to the single-bar plan that is so common in today's pubs and inns.

Above The inn has survived almost unaltered since the 15th century.

Above The Old Dog & Partridge was built in the 15th century.

STAFFORDSHIRE

OLD DOG & PARTRIDGE
TUTBURY

Not a pub for opponents of blood sports, the Dog & Partridge – even discounting its name! It was the inheritor of a tradition of bull-running reminiscent of Pamplona – but bloodier. Bull-running in medieval Tutbury was an annual entertainment laid on by the Brotherhood of Minstrels and the Prior of Tutbury. The Prior supplied the bull but, before it was set loose, its horns were cut off, its ears were cropped, its tail was docked, and pepper was blown up its nose. If the Minstrels managed to keep it in Staffordshire between sunrise and sunset, it was theirs. If it slipped past them and escaped across the Dove into Derbyshire, the Prior got to keep it.

Later, the more usual form of bull-baiting – you know, the one where the bull is chained to a ring securely set into a wall and then set upon by a pack of bull-dogs – replaced the bull-running, with the ring set into the wall of the Dog & Partridge. This form of light entertainment persisted until 1788. Later, the inn became – as well as a prominent posting-house on the London-Liverpool road – the headquarters of the Meynell Hunt. At this stage, the original half-timbered building, with its jettied upper storey, was extended to cope with its role as centre of local society.

Tutbury's castle was one the better-appointed prisons in which Mary Queen of Scots was imprisoned before the endless plots and conspiracies that surrounded her – and in which she happily participated – led to her final maximum-security incarceration and eventual execution at Fotheringhay. Even then, Burton, just down the road, was well-known for the quality of its ale. Mary's household is recorded as ordering its supplies from there in preference to whatever the Dog & Partridge was offering.

SUFFOLK

ANGEL
BURY ST EDMUNDS

O f all the great and grand coachings inns that survive, this must be among the very greatest and grandest. But the classical mansion you now see stands on much older foundations.

The present building was completed in 1779 to replace an earlier Angel, which was an amalgam of three separate inns dating to the 15th century. These were the original Angel, built in 1452 as a guest-house for the Abbey opposite; the Castle, first mentioned in 1418; and the White Bear, later the Boar's Head.

The Angel and the Castle were merged in 1533; in 1537 they and the Boar's Head were bequeathed jointly to the Guildhall to fund church repairs and curates' stipends. The whole parcel was sold in 1582 as a single inn, called the Angel, to a Mr Potter; his grand-daughter gave it back to the Guildhall 35 years later; and the Angel then remained in public possession until 1917.

The Angel ran its first coach in 1739, and did well on the trade for more than a century, with mail coaches and post-chaises on the London-Norwich road stopping there. A new service, the Surprise, was started as late as 1840. It took six hours from London to Bury. This coach, along with the Old Bury and the Hope, was still running to the Bull at Bishopsgate, in 1880.

Dickens knew the place well. Here, Pickwick, bedridden with rheumatism, learnt of Mrs Bardell's lawsuit; here, Pickwick and Sam Weller met Job Trotter: "'And this,' said Mr Pickwick, 'is the Angel!'"

The ground below is supposedly riddled with passages and tunnels: in the 19th century, a fiddler set out to explore them, playing his violin so his friends above could track him. The music grew fainter and became inaudible; the fiddler was never seen again.

Above The Angel has a grand portico and balcony.

GREAT WHITE HORSE
IPSWICH

Some people and places are only famous because someone more famous has poked fun at them. Who would have heard of East Cheam if Tony Hancock hadn't made it his radio home? Who would have heard of Des O'Connor if Morecambe & Wise had not lampooned him weekly on national TV? And who would have heard of the Great White Horse Inn if Dickens had not hated it so?

Dickens knew the inn from his days as a political reporter, having covered an election in Ipswich. By then, the old inn had passed its best, as coaching gave way to rail travel.

"The Great White Horse," wrote Dickens, "is famous in the neighbourhood in the same degree as a prize ox or county-paper chronicled turnip or unwieldy pig – for its enormous size. Never were there such labyrinthine uncarpeted passages, such clusters of mouldy ill-lighted rooms, such huge numbers of small dens for eating and sleeping in beneath any one roof as are collected together between the four walls of the Great White Horse at Ipswich."

Dickens went on to describe a miserable fire, an hour's wait for a meal, and a waiter with a fortnight-old napkin, and was perfectly withering about the admittedly energetic sculpting of a white horse that surmounts the inn porch, which was "rendered more conspicuous by a stone statue of some rampacious animal with flowing mane and tail distantly resembling an insane cart-horse."

Well, the best of satire has some truth in it; reading between the lines, one makes out a portrait of the typical late-Georgian facade and, behind it, the equally typical warren of corridors and landings of a much older inn.

The inn is actually documented from 1518, and could be a good deal older. Here and there inside are bits and pieces of the original oak. By the 18th century, it was a considerable coaching inn. George II broke a journey from Lowestoft to London here in 1737;

Nelson stayed in 1800; and Louis XVIII of France twice feasted here during his exile in Britain.

But Dickens didn't like it, and set one of the more embarrassing episodes of the *Pickwick Papers* here, when Mr Pickwick mistook his room in the dark and accidentally got into bed with the woman with yellow curl-papers. Yet, it was only the Dickens connection that saved the venerable inn from the bulldozer in the 1960s – an irony he would have appreciated.

Above The sculpture of a white horse above the door was ridiculed by Dickens.

SWAN
LAVENHAM

The Flemish weavers who migrated to East Anglia in the 14th century, on the initiative of Edward III and his Flemish queen, to found the English weaving industry can hardly have regretted leaving their homeland. For in England they became enormously wealthy. Lavenham, with its magnificent Perpendicular church, half-timbered Guildhall, and its streets of domestic architectural treasures, was one of the towns whose rise followed their arrival.

The Swan, first recorded in 1425, was once the home and workshop of the weavers who produced the cloth that clothed half of Christendom.

Above The yard was once used as a base for local carriers.

It stood on the corner of High Street and Water Street but, by 1667, had swallowed up both neighbouring houses and was mainly used by packmen, who toured the district collecting finished cloth. The inn had generous stabling and was solid enough to issue trade tokens.

A century later, the Swan was an important coach stop, home of the Lavenham Machine, advertised in 1764 as leaving the Swan at 5am every Monday, Wednesday and Friday for the Spread Eagle in Gracechurch Street, London; and leaving the Spread Eagle at 6am every Tuesday, Thursday and Saturday at 11 shillings a passenger, or 5s 6d for outsiders and babes in arms. Passengers were allowed 20lbs of luggage. The stables also put up post-chaises on the London-Bury road. It was a pretty sizeable undertaking: an 1830 bill of sale lists six parlours, two kitchens, four cellars, 12 bedrooms, a brewhouse, and stabling for 50 horses.

When railways killed the coach trade, the inn dwindled to no more than a beerhouse. The creation of Trust Houses in the early part of this century was the saviour of the Swan. In 1933, a tawdry Victorian brick front was removed, the guest rooms were reopened, and the old arch became the main entrance. During the Second World War, the newly restored inn was a magnet for USAAF and RAF bomber crews from the many surrounding airfields. It is impossible to look on the autographs and mementos they left without wondering how many of them never came back.

In the 1960s, Trust Houses expanded the inn by buying a row of shops in Water Street and the medieval Wool Hall in Lady Street. The hall had been dismantled in 1911, and sold to Princess Louise, who intended to re-erect it at Ascot, but a local outcry concerted by the conservationist Henry Taylor persuaded her to return it and it was, for a time, used as a hostel for women railway workers.

At the same time that the inn was being expanded, the old yard was made into today's cloistered garden, setting the seal on an inn which, according to one travel writer of the 1970s, "with its profusion of timbers, oak beams and studs, jettied gables and glowing red-tiled roofs, is unarguably the most sumptuous the region has to offer."

Overleaf The Swan started life as a row of three houses.

BULL

LONG MELFORD

Long Melford was a wool town, and the Bull started life as a weaver's home and workshop. It is probably rather older than the Swan – possibly mid-14th century, since a black bull was a supporter of Edward III's arms – and probably became an inn in the late 16th century, when weaving was declining. It was at this time that the rear gallery, of which traces can still be seen, was added, and the old hall was divided into two floors and equipped with flues and chimneys to replace the standard medieval form of ventilation – a hole in the roof.

Throughout the Bull are carved timbers of unusual richness: the joists supporting the roof of the lounge crawl with acanthus, or its 15th-century equivalent, and, on one spandrel, is a splendid Tudor wose – not a Tudor rose, a Tudor wose, or wood sprite. The carving is a trenchant reminder that 16th-century folk really believed in bogles and boggarts. A walk in the woods was very much spookier for Shakespearian man than it would be for you or me – ironic, given that Shakespearian man had to spend very much more time in the woods than you and I do.

The main doorcase carries the date 1649 and the initials WD for Walter Drew, one of three generations of Drews to own the pub. In 1648, Roger Greene was hanged for the murder, in a pub brawl here, of Richard Evered. Either Greene or Evered still walks, doing the door-slamming, dog-frightening, psychic-titillating things that revenants do.

Long Melford lives up to its name. It straggles out for more than a mile along a wide road, which probably originated as a drovers' route, headed for the livestock markets of London and, which, in the 18th century, became a convenient coach-route. The Bull, with its galleried courtyard, was an important stop on the London-Bury-Norwich route. Like the Swan at Lavenham, it decayed considerably once the coaches were superseded by rail; also like the Swan, it was revived by Trust Houses, which removed an ugly Victorian stucco front. Like the Swan again, it is now as perfect an English inn as you could wish.

Above The jettied front was uncovered when Trust Houses took over the inn.

Above Burford Bridge Hotel is still popular with people touring the Downs.

SURREY

BURFORD BRIDGE HOTEL
BOX HILL

Sited picturesquely at the foot of Box Hill's steep and wooded slopes and strategically at a crossing of the River Mole, the Burford Bridge Hotel got off to a flying start in life and has remained well up-market ever since.

Originally a private house, it was turned into an inn in the 1770s when a new bridge was built over the Mole to carry the London-Brighton road through a gap in the Downs hitherto impassable to wheeled traffic in winter. Only the mullioned rear windows are left of the original, which took over the licence and the name of a neighbouring alehouse, the Fox & Hounds.

Being a convenient distance from London, it quickly became a regular halt for travellers by public coach and private chaise. Owing to its romantic setting, it soon found favour with trippers too, for whom pleasure gardens were specially created. Nelson and Lady Hamilton dallied here for a few days in 1801 and again in 1802; other visitors included Wordsworth, Southey, Hazlitt and Princess Victoria, who, before her accession, seems to have stayed at more inns than Elizabeth I.

It wasn't only travellers who relished this scenic spot: some came for longer. Keats completed 'Endymion' here, dating it "Burford Bridge, November 28 1817". In 1878, RL Stevenson wrote much of his *New Arabian Nights* at the Burford Bridge Hotel, as it had by then become, returning to stay in 1882 while visiting his friend George Meredith who lived in a cottage nearby.

The ballroom was, until 1935, when it was taken apart and moved, a 17th-century tithe barn at Abinger. On a bracket in the minstrel's gallery stands a small terracotta Mr Punch – strange things are said to happen if this is moved.

WHITE HORSE
DORKING

The White Horse is one of the few historic buildings in Dorking High Street to have survived the post-war town planners – which is just as well, since it is probably the oldest building in town.

Dorking was a town in Saxon times, standing at the junction of Stane Street, which linked London with Chichester, and the North Downs Way, an Iron Age trade route that took on a new lease of life as the Pilgrim's Way. It was also the county's main market town.

The site on which the White Horse now stands was occupied in 1278 by a hospice belonging to the Knights of St John, known as Cross House. The English branch of the Order was suppressed by Henry VIII at the time of the Dissolution of the monasteries. Cross House, however, did not retain its role as a guest-house and remained in ecclesiastical use. The present front was added in about 1700: behind it lies much 15th- and 16th-century fabric, but the rock-hewn cellars (which include a well) are much older and are undoubtedly the foundations of the original Cross House.

The Vicarage turned inn in 1750, when the coach trade was growing, taking its name from arms of the Dukes of Norfolk, who were also lords of the manor of Dorking. Big new stables and a new coach arch were built over the old Vicarage gardens.

Later on, Dickens visited Dorking in his role as a political journalist. Argument has raged over which inn was the original for the Marquis of Granby in *The Pickwick Papers*, the King's Head (now demolished) or the White Horse. The truth is that Dickens, like all novelists, took a little here and a little there and topped it all up from his imagination.

A curious postscript to the history of coaching is that in the Edwardian period a coach and four ran every day during the summer between Charing Cross and the White Horse, purely for the tourists. If anyone tried it now they'd soon find that the contest between horse-drawn coach and articulated lorry is a desperately uneven one.

Above For generations, the White Horse served as the town's vicarage.

BUSH
FARNHAM

Despite its ivy-clad Georgian front, broad stableyard and extensive gardens, the Bush has always had the bad luck to be eclipsed by a comparatively humble pub in the town, the Jolly Farmer. This is purely because the smaller of the two was the birthplace of the early 19th-century radical MP, journalist and farmer William Cobbett, author of *Cottage Economy* and *Rural Rides* among many other works. But people who visited Farnham to pay tribute at Cobbett's shrine – it was even called the William Cobbett for a while in the 1960s – inevitably stayed at the Bush while they were there. Cobbett himself, reminiscing in later years over his childhood at the Jolly Farmer, did so (Thomas Burke informs us) from the comfortable vantage-point of the Bush.

A medieval foundation, the Bush sheltered travellers on the Pilgrim's Way, which passes through the town, and also functioned as a guest-house for the many high-ranking clergy visiting Farnham Castle to pay court to the Bishops of Winchester, who resided there throughout the Middle Ages, having built it after the Norman Conquest.

Farnham stands where the road for Bagshot, Staines and London splits from the Pilgrim's Way. It became an important stop on several coach-routes, and was extensively redeveloped to cope with the increase in traffic. During the course of alterations in 1903 a staircase leading to the rafters in the oldest part of the inn was uncovered. The discovery prompted romantics to speculate that the staircase was a bolt-hole used by highwaymen evading capture.

Nice as the story is, it's unlikely to be true. It's not unusual in such places to discover rooms that have not seen the light of day since the 18th or 19th centuries. One explanation is that builders of the time found it cheaper and easier, when extending rambling old buildings, to wall off awkward nooks and crannies rather than try to incorporate them into the strictly-proportioned plan demanded by neo-classical taste.

Previous pages The Bush is one of the grandest of England's fine old inns.

SUSSEX

WHITE HART
LEWES

B ehind a rather ordinary classical frontage is hidden the rambling timber-framed house of the Pelham family, built for them in the 16th century. The Pelhams were destined for higher things. In 1653 they moved out of their house and, in 1717, the year that they were elevated to the Duchy of Newcastle, the house became an inn. The name was inherited from a much earlier tavern some way down the street, from which the licence was transferred.

The first landlord, Richard Verrall, was one of the pioneers of the coaching trade, and the White Hart quickly became Lewes' principal inn, much in demand for assemblies, balls and election dinners. Verrall's son William, author of *The Compleat System Of Cookerie*, inherited it in 1737 and was landlord until his death in 1761, upon which the inn was sold to Thomas Scrace.

Under Scrace the business continued to flourish: the County Court was held in a panelled room upstairs, and the Flying Machine left at 6am every Monday and Thursday for the Golden Cross, Charing Cross, returning on Tuesdays and Saturdays. Scrace also tolerated the doings of a group of young radicals who called themselves the Headstrong Club and included a young customs officer called Tom Paine, later the author of *The Rights Of Man*. Looking back on his youthful days there he was to remark that the White Hart was "the cradle of the American Revolution".

In 1822 another radical, William Cobbett, spent the night here on his Rural Rides; and in 1929 the Labour Foreign Secretary Arthur Henderson chose the inn for a meeting with a Soviet envoy, Mr Dorgalevski, following which, diplomatic relations between Britain and the Soviet Union were restored. The Tories were outraged: referring to

the inn's long association with Sussex County Cricket Club, Stanley Baldwin sarcastically remarked: "I think the Foreign Secretary was playing a straight bat very carefully; but after lunching with the Soviet representatives, he collapsed," adding: "To those whom it may concern, you get the best of ale there."

Above The White Hart became an inn in 1717.

SPREAD EAGLE
MIDHURST

"That old and most revered of all prime inns of this world," as Hilaire Belloc described the Spread Eagle in 1912, dates back to about 1430 when the the oldest part of the present building with its jettied first floor was built to replace a hunting lodge of the Bohuns, lords of the manor since 1190.

In its earliest days, the building accommodated a row of shops on the West Street frontage, and in the 16th century unusually became both a tavern and an inn. It evidently did well: Elizabeth I lodged here while she was visiting Cowdray Park in 1591 and was entertained "marvellously, nay excessively".

In the mid-17th century, the inn was greatly extended, acquiring a new set of stables to accommodate travellers through this junction of north-south and east-west routes. It was clearly doing well, issuing its own trade tokens when small change was in short supply in the later 17th century.

By 1730 the Spread Eagle's insurance value was £1,000, a very substantial sum in those days, and it had begun to capture much of the coach trade on the London-Chichester road. It maintained this trade for 150 years and was one of the country's last functioning coaching inns, as Midhurst was not on the railway until the 1880s.

In 1907 the Spread Eagle was one of the first old coaching inns to open a garage (demolished in 1966 to enlarge the car park); its prime status was proved by a visit in 1909 from an ailing Edward VII. Its proximity to Goodwood racecourse accounted for some of the high-spending custom including, in 1939, Goering and Ribbentrop. Ostensibly there for the racing, they went to the Leonardslee estate at Horsham, which Goering fancied as a post-invasion country seat.

The three obligatory ghosts are a coachman in an upstairs room, a golden lady in the residents' lounge, and a girl in a green Tudor dress in one of the bars.

Overleaf The Spread Eagle still provides race-goers with a convenient place to stay.

GEORGE

RYE

Everyone knows the quaint, rambling, late medieval Mermaid in Rye, with its priest's hole and stories of smugglers. But the Mermaid was always more of a tavern than an inn: the principal inn was always the George.

The neo-classical front with its imposing portico masks a Tudor building, as the exposed beams inside prove. Rye in Tudor times, before the Rother estuary silted up, was a major port and the base of the Lords Warden of the Cinque Ports at a time when the whole south-east coast was open to French raids.

The George achieved its head inn status in the 18th century, when it acquired its facade, its Long Room, and a well-known coach service, the Diligence, which ran to London and back on alternate days right up to 1845. The inn was also a centre for municipal affairs: the Long Room witnessed many civic banquets and entertained important military visitors, including the Duke of Wellington, on tours of inspection.

Annual mayoral dinners have been held in the Long Room since the early 19th century, and it has long been the custom for the newly elected mayor to fling a shovelful of hot pennies from its balcony to the crowds below.

The balcony was also traditionally used to declare the results of Parliamentary elections. Rye was the scene of a notorious case of electoral malpractice in 1852 when one candidate, Alexander McKinnon, hosted a lavish banquet in the Long Room for the handful of property-owners who in those days made up the electoral roll of the borough. This was blatant bribery and utterly illegal. McKinnon tried to dodge the rules by claiming his predecessor in the seat had footed the bill, not him. Then a witness came forward saying he had seen McKinnon leaving the huge sum of £230 under a bench in another pub to be collected by an intermediary and handed to McKinnon's election agent, Jeremiah Smith, who then paid for the banquet. It turned out that

Smith and McKinnon had illegally bought drinks for the voters and mob on a huge scale. Smith was tried, convicted, and got 12 months. But he showed such smooth plausibility that he managed to persuade the jurors who had found him guilty to petition against their own verdict on the grounds that they had been misled by the prosecution. McKinnon was subsequently pardoned!

Above The George – a well known building in Rye for hundreds of years.

WARWICKSHIRE

SHAKESPEARE
STRATFORD-ON-AVON

Stratford is a town of fine old Elizabethan pubs and inns, and one of them just had to be called the Shakespeare. Fortunately, it lives up to its billing.

The Shakespeare is two buildings: one of the 15th century, originally the Great House; the other a century or so younger, originally the Five Gables. The Great House was built by Sir Hugh Clopton in 1486 and has a link with Shakespeare: Sir Hugh's descendants owned New Place, which Shakespeare rented in the 1590s; he or his agent must have visited the Great House to pay the rent.

The Great House was damaged in the Civil War and was partly rebuilt in brick with a plastered front. It appears to have been turned into an inn soon after, and was expanded to incorporate the Five Gables in the 18th century. Tradition has it that the greatest Shakespearian of them all, David Garrick, suggested naming the rooms after Shakespeare's plays in 1796 when he was in Stratford to perform the official opening of the new town hall. The snug bar is called Measure For Measure, the dining-room is As You Like It, the bridal suite is Venus & Adonis, and so on. One presumes there is a room called Hamlet for guests who substitute endless introspection for action. ("To shower before dinner, or not to shower before dinner; that is the question ...")

The inn was substantially altered in a long restoration project that started in 1880: both the 17th-century brick front and a *porte-cochere* of about 1820 were removed, and four new gables were added to the old Great House to match the roof of the Five Gables.

In 1934 the King of Jordan stayed at the Shakespeare when he visited Stratford and a throng of curious Warwickshire folk gathered to watch this Near Eastern exotic's stately progress to the theatre.

Previous pages It took 40 years to make the alterations to the Shakespeare.

WILTSHIRE

WAGGON & HORSES
BECKHAMPTON

P uzzling over which inns Dickens drew on for inspiration was one of the great literary hobbies of the 1920s and '30s, when literati happily let the trees hide the wood. This is the leading contender for the inn on the Marlborough Downs in the Bagman's Tale in Chapter 14 of *The Pickwick Papers*, although many have pleaded the causes of the Black Horse at Cherhill, the Ailesbury Arms at Manton, and a long-gone drovers' inn, the Shepherds Shore on Wansdyke.

All one can say for certain is that Dickens came this way in 1835, saw many inns, liked much of what he saw, and used what he liked for his own purposes. The thing is to come to the Waggon & Horses in the spirit in which Dickens came: not to search too assiduously for physical characteristics that tally with the charming story of Tom Smart, but to seek the elements that really mattered to the love-starved novelist: good company, good cheer, and good things in plenty.

Certainly to Harper, this was the right place: "The Waggon & Horses is just the house a needy bagman would have selected," he wrote. "It was in coaching days a homely yet comfortable inn that received those travellers who did not relish either the state or the expense of the great Beckhampton Inn opposite where the post-horses were kept and the very elite of the roads resorted."

The Great Western Railway opened in 1841, and the Beckhampton Inn was speedily ruined, becoming a racing stables. The Waggon & Horses, built in Tudor times with the materials that came most readily to hand – in this case sarsens from the stone circle and avenue at Avebury nearby – survived.

The pub is strategically sited at the junction of two ancient routes, and throughout its history its location ensured a steady trade. Some of the coaches on the London-Bath road changed horses here, but its main custom came from the juggernauts of the 17th and 18th centuries: the great, slow freight wagons with their 8ft wheels. The inn even had a smithy where the huge carthorses could be shod, and at one time there were enormous stables where the wagons and their cargoes could be secured overnight while the carters slept in the haylofts above.

Before banks became widely established, wagoners had to travel with large quantities of cash. Not surprisingly, the lonely roads around Beckhampton were infested with highwaymen, many of whom ended up swinging from the gibbet next to the inn or its twin on Inkpen Beacon. If that is not eerie enough for you, Beckhampton is a great centre for exploring the prehistoric landscape of Wiltshire: Avebury, Silbury, and the Kennett barrows are close at hand, and Stonehenge is not a long drive.

Above The Waggon & Horses, with its thatched roof, is a welcome sight to travellers.

BEAR
DEVIZES

The Bear owes its fortune to the highwaymen who plagued the turnpike over the Marlborough Downs. The gibbet proved so poor a deterrent that in the 1780s the authorities were forced to find an entirely new route for the London-Bath road. Consequently the southern route through Devizes was upgraded and the old road across the Downs was virtually abandoned. Before long, there were as many as 30 coaches a day stopping at the Bear.

Even before the new road and its welcome traffic, the Bear had been the town's principal inn. First recorded in 1599, the property included a large public hall where the Corn Exchange now stands, a big yard known as the Queen's Stables, and a bear garden used for bull and bear-baiting. An 18th-century landlord, John Watley, was well known throughout the region. He established a dining club called the Bear Club, which evolved into a charitable trust raising funds for scholarships for local children. Watley's sucessor, Thomas Lawrence was to become even better known. A failed articled clerk, failed poet, and failed actor, Lawrence had previous-

Above The Bear has seen many famous characters come and go.

ly run the Coffee House in Bristol. He took over the Bear in 1772, but is more renowned for his son's achievements than for his own.

Lawrence won the gratitude of travellers for marking the road across the Downs with six-foot poles – a boon in winter – and for his "warm rooms and soft beds"; but it was his son-prodigy who attracted the attention of commentators such as Fanny Burney, who was travelling to Bath with Mrs Thrale in 1780 and spent the night at the Bear. As they played whist, they heard music from next door and, on enquiring, discovered that the musicians were the innkeeper's daughters. His son, Thomas, was away, but they saw his drawings "that were really beautiful".

As a five-year-old, not only could Lawrence jnr. recite great chunks of Milton, he could also draw remarkable portraits, for which his father charged the princely sum of 10s 6d. Dr Johnson, Garrick, Burke, Sheridan and Mrs Siddons were among those inveigled into parting with half a guinea by Lawrence père's "obtrusive pertinacity". The family ended up quitting the Bear and living on Thomas' earnings. By 1820 he was president of the Royal Academy and was knighted by George IV.

The Lawrences left the inn just before the turnpike was moved to pass through Devizes. Under the Halcombe family who succeeded them, the Bear rose to a peak of prosperity. A new wing was built, and patrons included George III and Queen Charlotte in 1789. Queen Charlotte stayed again in 1817, remarking that she had had a most elegant repast and that the inn had put at her disposal 10 pairs of horses as fine as any put in traces.

Long after the demise of coaching, the Bear maintained its premier status in the district: it had been the headquarters of the county militia since 1758, and here in 1893 the officers entertained the Prince of Wales, Prince Arthur of Connaught, and Prince Edward of Saxe-Coburg when they reviewed the troops.

Devizes pie, a speciality of the house, was taken from a recipe of 1836 which included calf's head and brains, pickled tongue, sweetbreads, lamb, veal, bacon, and boiled eggs spiced with cayenne. Go on ... try it – it may not still contain all these!

WHITE HART

SALISBURY

The White Hart is not one of Salisbury's most ancient inns but it is a fine example of the way that many inns were torn down and rebuilt in the classical style in the Georgian period.

The White Hart replaced a building first recorded in the late 15th century, in which Sir Walter Raleigh met James I after the failure of his disastrous Guyana expedition in 1618. It had been Raleigh's last chance and he had been released from prison to mount the expedition. His backers were badly out of pocket and he knew what trouble he was in. In an unsuccessful attempt to deflect the royal wrath he feigned leprosy and hid in his room, pretending to fast but actually sending a servant down to the kitchen for bread and mutton. Nothing mollified the monarch, who sent the knight first to the Tower and then to the block.

Another visitor in similarly melancholy circumstances was the American revolutionary leader Henry Laurens, captured at sea in 1780 en route to a diplomatic mission in Europe. He was held here overnight on his way to a 14-month stretch in the Tower.

By that time the White Hart had become a prosperous coaching inn, the home of the Salisbury Stage Coach and running "neat four-wheeled chaises" for 9d a mile. By 1800 it had seen off the competition from the 14th-century George, which closed in 1796 and whose facade is preserved in a shopping mall, and it was decided to take on the challenge of the Antelope by rebuilding in the grand style.

The new building was easily imposing enough to be a town hall or middle-ranking country house. The centrepiece of a rather severe front is a portico of four Ionic pillars topped by a pediment upon which was

placed, in 1827, a magnificent sculpture of the inn's eponymous beast. All that remains of the earlier inn is a short piece of timber to which is tacked a scrap of hessian painted with gold acanthus on a blue background. The remnant is thought to be part of a mid-Tudor wall-painting.

Above The imposing portico of the White Hart.

WORCESTERSHIRE

LYGON ARMS
BROADWAY

It is difficult to believe that this gem – no, this tiara, for a gem suggests something small – in the crown jewels of England's historic inns was, a century ago, in desperate financial straits, reduced to the status of a village beerhouse. Yet it was so; and the fact that this most peerless inn now belongs to the august Savoy Group is proof positive that the wheel of fortune turns and turns.

This beautiful house of golden stone was built in 1620 by John and Ursula Trevis, whose names are carved over the door. John died in 1641 and has a brass in the church. The inn was then the White Hart, and had replaced an inn of that name that is first recorded in 1540. Cromwell was its first celebrity guest: in 1651 he spent the eve of the battle of Worcester here. By dinner-time next day the second civil war was over, Charles II was in full romantic flight; and Parliament's General was assured as England's ruler for the remaining seven years of his life. The room he stayed in has a notable fireplace with plaster mantel, probably the work of itinerant Italian craftsmen.

Broadway, a long and straggling village at the foot of the Cotswolds, became a stopping point on the road from London to Worcester and beyond. Teams travelling from London were glad to stop and rest after the arduous descent of Fish Hill;

Right American Henry Ford was a fan of the Lygon Arms.

teams from Worcester were glad to stop and gather strength before it. After Waterloo the inn came into the hands of the Lygon family, newly created Earls Beauchamp, and a former family servant, Old Mullins, became its landlord, changing the inn's name to honour his patron. But the end of coaching hit the Lygon hard. It scraped along as the headquarters of the local hunt for a few lean decades then belonged briefly to a local brewery. It was eventually rescued from dereliction in 1903 by perhaps the greatest innkeeper-pioneer of his generation: Sidney Bolton Russell.

Russell deserves a chapter to himself. A motor enthusiast who combined taste and vision with the necessary resources, he latched on to the commercial potential of Merrie England and filled the ancient shell he had bought with carefully collected antiques and, indeed, antiquities. (He also stripped out the sash windows with which some Victorian vandal had replaced the original mullions.)

Not only priceless pieces of furniture, but also an entire inglenook fireplace were imported from country house sales, "the spoil of curiosity shops", and elsewhere until the Lygon Arms became a homing beacon for visitors from all over the world, who appreciated Russell's fulsome version of the English aesthetic. Indeed Broadway itself, according to Thomas Burke, was an unexceptional colony of artists, potters and other urban refugees remarkable only for the Lygon Arms. Russell was not afraid to build anew, either: he had today's great hall designed in 1909, and it was pronounced "perfect" by the architectural critic Pevsner.

The Lygon Arms remained in family hands through two more generations. Today it is a palace of inns in a region reckoned by many to be the loveliest in the land. In the 18th century the hyper-critical Viscount Torrington said: "There cannot be a cleaner, civiller inn than this," and in the 1950s the cricket writer Denzil Batchelor described it as "not a period piece, but a period masterpiece". Both were right.

TALBOT
STOURBRIDGE

The plain, red-brick front of the Talbot in Stourbridge's High Street gives few clues as to the treasures within – well, it gives two clues, to be precise, because a close inspection of the arch will reveal that the gateposts are made of a single tree split in half and left rough.

A look around the yard with its trellised galleries, half-timbered gables and Tudor windows tells the old story – the brick front is a late Georgian addition to a much older inn. Just how old, though, is uncertain. The first reliable record of the inn is in 1685 when, on 20 December: "Samuel Foley, Batchelor of Divinity, leased to Jonathan Pryke of Stourbridge, Innholder, for 21 years, the house in the High Street of Stourbridge by the name of The Talbot for the yearly rent of £18."

Two of the inn's internal features may be of this date or even earlier. They are a narrow wooden staircase of several short flights, with a heavy oak banister rail supported on simply turned balustrades, and the old coffee room. This last is a large upstairs room with a low moulded plaster ceiling. It is panelled from top to bottom and contains a great fireplace whose carved mantelpiece depicts Abraham offering up Isaac. This was where the best guests were shown in the Talbot's heyday; perhaps it was also the meeting place of the Friendly Society of Tradesmen, a forerunner in spirit of today's Rotary, that had its headquarters at the inn in 1768. No one over 40 was admitted, nor anyone earning less than 9 shillings a week, nor any "bumbailiff or bumbailiff's follower".

Above Edward VIII, as Prince of Wales, lunched at the Talbot in 1928.

YORKSHIRE

ROYAL OAK
DACRE BANKS

All you could ask for in a country inn, the Royal Oak has. Set on the edge of the Yorkshire Dales, its stout stone walls enclose a complex of cosy wood-panelled snugs and a gracious dining-room where the fine food is more than matched by the quality of the ale.

There was probably an inn on the site when Dacre Banks belonged to Fountains Abbey in the Middle Ages. After the Dissolution, Dacre came into the possession of the Ingilby family of nearby Ripley Castle, whose bailiff would set himself up in state at the Royal Oak on quarter-days to collect the rents of the family's tenants in the district.

The present inn is dated 1752, although the coach-house is a little older. As well as local coaches and other horse-traffic, the inn was used by drovers bringing cattle and sheep down from Wharfedale. All this traffic was superseded by the railway, which arrived in the 1840s but did the Royal Oak no harm: this was the nearest stop to Brimham Rocks, so the influx of trippers far outweighed the loss of the previous trade.

In an interesting twist of fate, the Royal Oak, having had its links with Rome forcibly severed in the Dissolution, had them restored after the Emancipation three centuries later. Local Roman Catholics were allowed to hear Mass in an upstairs room – though one wonders whether they proved good customers in the bar afterwards.

Like many country inns, the Royal Oak had its own smallholding, in this case a plot of 24 acres. The whole lot was sold as a single parcel by the Ingilby family in 1919 to pay death duties, but the farm buildings were later sold on and demolished and there is now a garage on the site.

Left The Royal Oak provided convenient accommodation for visitors to Yorkshire.

BLACK SWAN HOTEL
HELMSLEY

Founded in the 16th century, the stone-built Black Swan has come a long way since it was a staging-post for the trade in Ryedale fleeces. Then, it was pack-horses that thronged the yard, but they necessitated the construction of stables, which came into good use in the 18th century when Helmsley's position at the junction of the roads connecting York, Scarborough and Teesside made it an important coaching town. The Black Horse shared the trade with the Crown, but did well enough to enjoy the addition of the standard classical frontage.

By the time of the demise of the coaching trade, Helmsley had also developed as a centre for tourism in the Yorkshire Dales, ensuring not only the inn's survival but its expansion. From coaching inn it mutated into country hotel; but as well as lodging visitors to the region, it was also a hub of local society. The Sunnington foxhounds met here regularly, and the tenants of Lord Feversham of Duncombe Hall held their annual rent dinner in its dining room. To dignify the hotel, Jacobean panelling was imported from the church in 1860, and a Tudor doorway was rescued from the ruins of Helmsley Castle and installed at the top of the cellar steps.

After the Second World War, the Black Swan engaged in a further programme of expansion. In 1947, it took over the next-door Georgian house with its elegantly curving staircase, and seven years later the Tudor vicarage next to that. It now occupies the whole of one side of the square.

Left The Black Swan has an affectionate nickname – the Mucky Duck.

GOLDEN LION
NORTHALLERTON

Northallerton in the late 18th century was not only a stage on the Great North Road, it was also a considerable market town with a large and well established annual horse fair. And, in the grand Georgian Golden Lion, it has an inn to match its status.

In the cellar you will find ancient masonry and Tudor brickwork, but the original inn was almost entirely demolished and rebuilt in the mid-18th century, for the Golden Lion's days of greatness began with coaching. It was the next stop on the Great North Road after Thirsk, and the landlord in the early 19th century, Francis Hirst, supplied horses both to the mails and to private coaches on two stages amounting to about 23 miles.

Even before the royal mail switched from post-horses to coaches in 1784, the Golden Lion was the post-office for the district: post-boys' quarters above the stables were converted into staff flats in only the 1930s. The inn lived not just on coaching and the mails, though: succeeding owners diversified into other areas of horse-coping, and at the annual fair horses were run up and down a yard more than 100 yards long to show their paces to prospective buyers. The extensive stables were also used from 1765 as loose-boxes by owners entering horses at Northallerton races, a lucrative sideline for the inn's owners. It was an expensive place in those days. Referring to it as a fictitious Black Swan, Sidney Smith warned against staying too long there, or "your bill will come to £1,000, beside the waiter."

Inside, the Assembly Room occupies the front of the first floor, and there are small-paned early Georgian windows with window-seats, old grates, and a locally made coaching clock.

Right The Golden Lion gets its name from the arms of the local Percy family.

BOAR'S HEAD

RIPLEY

Can there be such a thing as a new inn? If you accept that part of the requirement of an inn is a hefty dose of history and tradition, it would seem hard for a newcomer to fit the bill. The Boar's Head in Ripley does – but it cheats.

Ripley is an 18th-century model village, built as a companion to the castle and, like the castle, the property of the Ingilby family. Until the early part of the century it had three inns including the Star, a posting-house of some local prominence and a stop for Leeds-Edinburgh coaches on the Great North Road.

Then in 1919 Sir William Ingilby, a stalwart of the church and evidently something of a temperance fanatic, inherited the castle. He seems not to have cared much for the poor man at his gate having a drink or two for, by such means as forbidding them to open on Sunday, he was eventually able to drive all three pubs out of business. The last landlord of the Star was Yorkshire and England cricketer Frank Smailes, who, upon receiving his eviction notice, threatened in reprisal to cut down the ancient virginia creeper which adorned the inn: Sir William had to take him to court to stop him.

Ripley was dry until 1990, when Sir Thomas Ingilby, a man of milder disposition than his ancestor, saw how ridiculous it was that such a popular tourist attraction should have no pub. He reopened the Star under the name the Boar's Head, a feature of the family crest since a 14th-century ancestor, also Thomas, rescued Edward III from a charging wild boar.

Don't leave the Boar's Head without trying Crackshot, an ale brewed specially for the inn by Daleside Brewery to a recipe of 1684 discovered in the castle library. The only omission from the original is the raw eggs – not really an ingredient, but used as finings before isinglass became widely known, and in today's climate of food safety hysteria, considered a little too risky.

Above The Boar's Head – an old inn with a new name.

UNICORN
RIPON

As the economic, social and religious capital of the central part of the Yorkshire Dales, Ripon has been an important settlement since at least the 7th century, when a monastery was founded here. The town received its charter in the late 9th century, and the Minster – although it has only had the status of a cathedral since 1836 – was built partly in the 12th century and partly in the 15th, on the site of a Saxon crypt.

The splendid Unicorn Hotel, dominating the Market Place, cannot boast such antiquity. It may be that one of the three breweries recorded in the poll tax return of 1379 was based on this site, but the Unicorn first comes into written history in the early 17th century when it was owned by Edward and Margaret Turner. The town's Corporation met in the inn, and Edward Alleyn, founder of Dulwich College in London, signed the conveyance on a property he was buying in Yorkshire "in the house of Margaret Turner at the sign of the Unicorn in Ripon" in 1626.

After Edward Turner's death in 1624, Margaret owned the Unicorn for another 23 years, witnessing an outbreak of plague in 1625, a civil war skirmish in the Market Place in 1642 and a brief visit by Charles I as prisoner of the Scots in 1647. Cromwell also stayed in the town twice, in 1648 and 1651 – maybe at the Unicorn.

In 1648, Margaret's son Thomas sold the Unicorn to Richard Porter, in whose family it remained for over 50 years. At this time the town Corporation was still meeting at the inn, which was listed in tax returns of 1672 as having eight hearths, making it a substantial establishment. An early 18th-century owner, Francis Cowling, was wealthy enough to donate a trophy to the local races.

In 1745, the sitting tenants, William and Sarah Haddon, bought the inn off the Cowlings for £410. The Haddons and their heirs presided over the Unicorn's heyday, when, although Ripon actually lies some miles off the Great North Road, many long-distance coaches including

Left Brick replaced the old timber front of the Unicorn.

the London-Newcastle Telegraph and the London-Glasgow mail, made detours to call at the inn. It was also the base for a number of local services.

During their profitable ownership of the Unicorn, the Haddons expanded it to take over neighbouring buildings. Both magistrates' and coroner's courts sat at the inn, and the Turnpike Trust held its quarterly meeting here. There were rooms in the inn called the Breakfast Room, the Coffee Room, the Travellers' Room, the Bow Parlour, the Back Parlour, the Bar, the Taproom, and the Kitchen.

A servant of the Haddons, Tom Crudd, known as Old Boots, brought wider celebrity to the Unicorn thanks to a facial deformity that allowed him to hold a coin between his nose and his chin. In this manner, he accepted many tips from travellers, "it being no less satisfactory to him than entertaining to them". In 1793, by which time Crudd was dead and buried in the Minster yard, *Wonderful* magazine published an engraving from 1762 of him in characteristic attitude – slippers in one hand and boot-jack in the other. It has been so widely reproduced that even if you have never heard of Ripon or the Unicorn you are still likely to have seen Tom Crudd.

The Unicorn survived the arrival of the railway in 1848 more or less undiminished – indeed, as the railway brought tourists flocking to Fountains Abbey and the Dales, it actually increased the Unicorn's prosperity. Guests included Charles Luttwidge Dodgson, better known as Lewis Carroll, in 1858, and the Prince of Wales and his new bride – briefly – in 1863.

Above The sign of the Unicorn.

GOLDEN FLEECE
THIRSK

While the low ceilings and heavy beams inside the principal inn in Thirsk speak of a late Tudor or early Stuart ancestry, the Golden Fleece came into its own in the 1720s when it was run by a Mrs Lowery and was the land registry office for the North Riding. To Mrs Lowery's period of ownership belongs the older, lower part of the Golden Fleece, with the grand mantelpiece set into what used to be an open hearth 12ft wide, and the coffered ceiling of the old writing room.

During the 18th century the Golden Fleece and its rival, the Three Tuns, contended for the growing volume of coach traffic that passed through the town. There was plenty of business for both, as the Golden Fleece's enormous yard attests. But in 1815 the Three Tuns' landlady retired and handed its posting business on to her nephew George Blythe – who ran the Golden Fleece!

From this point the Golden Fleece enjoyed a brief but dramatic flowering, acquiring the taller of the buildings which now comprise the property as well as an unusually fine coaching clock, a collection of equestrian paintings, including an original JF Herring, and a set of good furniture much of which was still doing service in the 1930s.

George Blythe died in 1828, and the inn was jointly inherited by his nephew and great nephew, John and William Hall, who kept up to 60 coach-horses at a time in its capacious stables. When the railway came, the Golden Fleece continued to thrive. The railway brought more traffic with it than it superseded and there was still local trade, such as the weekly farmers' dinner, which continued until the last war, and the influx of thirsty punters stopping for a first drink between railway station and racecourse – and a last one on the way back.

Above The sign of the Golden Fleece

BLACK SWAN
YORK

Originally built in the 14th century, the Black Swan spent its first 300 years not as an inn but as a wealthy townhouse. It was home to the Bowes family – affluent merchants, leading local citizens and ancestors of the present Queen Mother. William Bowes represented York in four Parliaments under Henry V and VI, was sheriff of the city in 1407 and was mayor in 1417 and 1428. His son, also William, was mayor in 1443; and his son, Sir Martin, left York for London to become a goldsmith. In London he served as Lord Mayor in 1545 and became Court Jeweller to Queen Elizabeth I. Sir Martin never forgot York, though, and presented his native city with the Sword of State, which is still borne before its Lord Mayor on great occasions.

You would think it unlikely that such a prominent family had anything to do with papists, but tradition has it that Margaret Clitheroe, the Catholic martyr pressed to death under a door weighed down with stones for refusing to plead, was arrested in this very house. Interestingly, the inn's pride is a panelled upstairs room, probably the original family dining-room, which also hints at recusancy. The panelling in this room used to be covered from top to bottom with chiaroscuro paintings. But, by 1930, these had faded to little more than faint marks.

In that year an undamaged panel was found, revealing a painting of the Virgin Mary and St Elizabeth with Jesus and St John in a rustic landscape. If the rest of the paintings were on similar lines, they may well have been scrubbed out deliberately, either by the same Puritans who smashed the Minster's stained glass – or possibly by Roman Catholics who feared the paintings would betray them.

Above The Black Swan is one of York's major inns.

In 1683, the house came into the possession of Edward Thompson, Lord Mayor of York and a citizen of substance. He may have added the grand staircase and the parlour's moulded plaster ceiling, elegant door-cases and panelling.

In about 1715, the old house became a very superior inn: General Wolfe, the captor of Quebec, was born in it in 1727. Yet the Black Swan failed as a coaching inn, losing out to the better-sited, but now long-gone, George. In fact, it became a bit of a dive. An engraving of about 1800 shows a ramshackle porch tacked on, a layer of peeling stucco and some tottering chimney stacks. In 1884, a bricklayer conducted an auction at the pub: the only lot was his wife. He got 1s 6d for her. In 1900, a blacksmith was renting the yard as his forge: the horses were led through the main hall.

The inn was restored in 1930: the stucco was pulled off, missing timbers were replaced and the Black Swan became a smart town pub again.

Above The Black Swan has been restored to its fomer glory – inside and out.

INDEX

Ship & Bell, Horndean 100
Spread Eagle, Midhurst 205
Spreadeagle, Thame 163
Sun, Dedham 80
Sun, Hitchin 110
Swan, Bedford 28
Swan, Lavenham 190
Talbot, Mells 182
Talbot, Oundle 137
Talbot, Stourbridge 223

Three Swans, Market Harborough 122
Unicorn, Ripon 233
Unicorn, Stow-on-the-Wold 97
Waggon & Horses, Beckhampton 213
White Bull, Ribchester 120
White Hart, Lewes 203
White Hart, Salisbury 218

White Hart, St Albans 113
White Hart Royal, Moreton-in-Marsh 91
White Horse, Dorking 198
White Horse, Eaton Socon 47
White Horse, Romsey 103
Ye Olde Bell, Barnby Moor 144
Ye Olde Bell, Hurley 35

SUGGESTED FURTHER READING

Discovering Highwaymen, Russell Ash, Shire 1970.
The English Inn, Denzil Batchelor, Batsford 1963.
English Country Inns, Derry Brabbs, Weidenfeld & Nicolson 1986.
The English Inn, John Burke, Holmes & Meier 1981.
The English Inn, Thomas Burke, Longman 1930.
Inns & Their Signs, Eric R Delderfield, David & Charles 1975.
Dictionary of Pub Names, L Dunkling & G Wright, Routledge Kegan Paul 1987.
An Innkeeper's Diary, John Fothergill, Chatto & Windus 1931.
My Three Inns, John Fothergill, Chatto & Windus 1951.
Classic Country Pubs, Neil Hanson, Pavilion 1987.
The Old Inns of Old England vols I & II, Charles G Harper, Chapman Hall 1906.
Historic & Picturesque Inns of Old England, Charles G Harper, Burrow 1926.
The English Pub, Peter Haydon, Robert Hale 1994.
Tales of Old Inns, Richard Keverne, Collins 1939.
Old Country Inns, HP Maskell & EW Gregory, Pitman 1910.
The Ancient Roads of England, Jane Oliver, Cassell 1936.
The Village Pub, Roger Protz & Homer Sykes, Weidenfeld & Nicholson 1992.
The Old Inns of England, AE Richardson, Batsford 1934.
Discovering Horse-Drawn Carriages, DJ Smith, Shire 1975.
Inns of the Midlands, Norman Tiptaft, Tiptaft 1951.
Trust House Britain, Jean Wakeman, Hodder 1963.
Turnpike Roads, Geoffrey Wright, Shire 1992.